British Army Divisions in WWII

Part I: Armoured and Mixed Divisions

Trevor Laing

TRAVELOGUE 219

TL219-319 `British Army Divisions in WWII Part I: Armoured and Mixed Divisions', Edition 2, by Trevor Laing, January 2019
Published by: Travelogue 219
            Toronto, Canada
            www.tl219.com

ISBN 978-1-927679-80-7

Second Edition

Front cover photo: a Sherman tank in Belgium

Contents

Introduction

The study of British army divisions in World War II is interesting for several reasons; one of which is that the British didn't follow the sequential order that most nations did. Another reason is that some infantry divisions converted to mixed and mobile divisions in an effort to repeal an invasion. Added to the inconsistent numbers are divisions created for deception purposes only. Also, by the end of the war Britain experienced severe manpower shortages so they had to disband entire divisions to replace losses in other divisions.

The object of this series of books is to give a clear and concise listing of all the divisions that served in the British Army in World War II at any given time period. Several books have been published that provide this information, but I find that they can be difficult to read and/or only give part of the story. This series is designed for the reader to look up a division and go to the date that closest reflects the time period / battle that they are looking for. The date of each chart represents when its organization went through a change so all the reader has to do is go to the chart with the last change before the period that they are looking for.

Also provided is a history of each division, a description of their insignia and every unit that served in the division during World War II.

This book, Part I, focuses on the tanks in the British Army divisions and these were originally only in the new armoured divisions. Between May 1942 and January 1943 seven infantry divisions were converted to mixed divisions by exchanging one of their three infantry brigades for a tank brigade. It was one of the experiments that didn't really work out and by December 1943 all seven mixed divisions reverted back to a normal infantry division by exchanging the tank brigade for an infantry brigade. In all cases their original brigade was not available so another

1

brigade took its place. This explains the non-sequence numbering of the infantry brigades in these divisions.

The experimenting wasn't confided to the mixed divisions, the armoured divisions were constantly tinkering with their war establishment. A total of nine changes were made during the war and these didn't include all of the local changes that some divisions made. In some divisions, units came and went faster than they could be recorded. The following tries to capture all of the changes made to these divisions during World War II.

The Armoured Divisions

War Establishments:

There were nine changes to the armoured division's war establishment during the war and the reason for this is that the British Army had never operated an armoured division in action before and needed battle experience to balance the different arms in a division. However, before this balance could be reached the War Office tried several different arrangements and changed the war establishments frequently. These changes to the armoured divisions during the war were numerous and difficult to track. The armoured division started out with two armoured brigades, a support group that was light in artillery and engineers and a handful of divisional troops. It was a tank heavy arrangement because of the pre-war belief in "pure" armoured warfare; battles in the future would be tank vs. tank alone, exploiting the speed and mobility of the new weapon. The armoured division's mission was to seek out and destroy the enemy tank units. However this theory was to prove to be wrong and by the end of the war the support group was gone, more artillery and engineers added and one of the armoured brigades had been replaced with an infantry brigade. It is interesting to see how mixed brigade groups were attempted and disbanded during the war and then unofficially formed in divisions like the Guards Armoured Division towards the end of the war.

In an attempt to simply a division's components I have made seven charts that highlight the nine major changes as the British Army learned the most efficient combination of arms.

Where possible I have also included the type of tanks that each regiment had at the time. This may not be exact as some units used whatever they had at the time, including captured Italian tanks, and that this isn't an in-depth study of each formation. What the purpose of this book is to be a quick reference for each division at any given time period by the use of charts. For example: if a person wants to know the Guards Armoured Division's units during Operation Market Garden then all they have to do

<u>Typical Armoured Division May 1939</u>

Equipped with A9, A10 and A13 tanks and Vickers Light tanks

<u>Divisional Troops:</u>

Divisional Headquarters

Signals

Workshop RAOC

2 x Field Ambulance

4 x RASC Transport companies

<u>Light Armoured Brigade:</u>

Armoured Regiment: *2 Light Tank and 1 Cruiser Tank Squadrons*

Armoured Regiment: *2 Light Tank and 1 Cruiser Tank Squadrons*

Armoured Regiment: *2 Light Tank and 1 Cruiser Tank Squadrons*

<u>Heavy Armoured Brigade:</u>

Armoured Regiment: *3 Cruiser / Light Cruiser Squadrons*

Armoured Regiment: *3 Cruiser / Light Cruiser Squadrons*

Armoured Regiment: *3 Cruiser / Light Cruiser Squadrons*

<u>Support Group:</u>

Motor Battalion: *4 rifle companies*

Motor Battalion: *4 rifle companies*

Royal Artillery:

Field Artillery Regiment: *2 x 18-pdr or 25-pdr batteries*

Anti-tank/Lt. Anti-aircraft Regiment: *4 x 2-pdr / AA MG btys.*

Royal Engineers:

Field Squadron

Field Park Troop

Typical Armoured Division Autumn 1940

Divisional Troops:

Divisional Headquarters

Armoured Car Regiment (UK only)

Signals

Workshop RAOC

2 x Field Ambulances

4 x RASC Transport companies

Royal Engineers:

    Field Squadron

    Field Squadron

    Field Park Squadron

Armoured Brigade:

Armoured Regiment: *light and medium tanks*

Armoured Regiment: *light and medium tanks*

Armoured Regiment: *light and medium tanks*

Motor Battalion: 4 rifle companies

Armoured Brigade:

Armoured Regiment: *light and medium tanks*

Armoured Regiment: *light and medium tanks*

Armoured Regiment: *light and medium tanks*

Motor Battalion: *4 rifle companies*

Support Group:

Lorried Infantry Battalion

Royal Artillery:

    Field Artillery Regiment: *2 x 25-pdr batteries*

    Anti-tank/Lt. Anti-aircraft Regiment: *4 x 2-pdr/AA MG btys.*

is go to the chart for the Guards Armoured Division in 1944.

In Autumn 1940 and for the 4th time since 1938 the organization of an armoured division was changed. Now the division was to consist of six mixed regiments of light tanks and medium tanks, totally 320 tanks.

The next change was Genearl Auchinleck's new war establishment based on hard won experience gained during the winter fighting of 1941-42 in North Africa. It was designed to improve the cooperation of all of the arms in a division. One of the armoured brigades was replaced by a lorried infantry brigade while the other was made into a brigade group by adding artillery, infantry and engineers. The Support Group was eliminated because it was found that it often fought independently of the armour and never was in the support role.

The Brigade Group was short lived so this war establishment was changed within months of being put into action. The reason for this is because as soon as Lieutenant-General Bernard Montgomery took over command of the 8th Army in 1942 he put an end to the disastrous Brigade Group experiment and the result was the August 1942 version of the armoured division.

Further tinkering in April 1943 and then in March 1944 led to the war establishment that most of the divisions used their until the end of the war.

Typical Armoured Division Feb. 1942 (Middle East)

Divisional Troops:

Divisional Headquarters

Armoured Car Regiment

Signals

Workshop RAOC (REME)

2 x Field Ambulances

4 x RASC Transport companies

Royal Engineers:

Field Park Squadron

Armoured Brigade Group:

Armoured Regiment: *HQ Squadron and 3 Squadrons*

Armoured Regiment: *HQ Squadron and 3 Squadrons*

Armoured Regiment: *HQ Squadron and 3 Squadrons*

Motor Battalion: *4 rifle companies*

Field Artillery Regiment: *3 x 25-pdr batteries*

1 anti-tank battery: 16x2pdr/6pdr

Light AA Battery

Field Troop, RE

Motor Infantry Brigade Group:

Motor Infantry Battalion

Motor Infantry Battalion

Motor Infantry Battalion

Field Artillery Regiment: *3 x 25-pdr batteries*

1 anti-tank battery: 16x2pdr/6pdr

Light AA Battery

Field Squadron, RE (less 1 troop)

Typical Armoured Division May 1942 (UK)

Divisional Troops:

Divisional Headquarters

Armoured Car Regiment

Signals

Workshop RAOC (REME)

2 x Field Ambulances

4 x RASC Transport companies

Royal Artillery:

Field Artillery Regiment: *2 x 25-pdr batteries*

Field Artillery Regiment: *2 x 25-pdr batteries*

Anti-tank/Lt. Anti-aircraft Regiment: *4 x 2-pdr / AA MG btys.*

Royal Engineers:

Field Squadron

Field Squadron

Field Park Squadron

Armoured Brigade:

Armoured Regiment: *HQ Squadron and 3 Squadrons*

Armoured Regiment: *HQ Squadron and 3 Squadrons*

Armoured Regiment: *HQ Squadron and 3 Squadrons*

Motor Battalion: *4 rifle companies*

Infantry Brigade:

Infantry Battalion

Infantry Battalion

Infantry Battalion

<u>Typical Armoured Division August 1942 (Middle East)</u>

<u>Divisional Troops:</u>

Divisional Headquarters

Armoured Car Regiment

Signals

Workshop RAOC /REME

2 x Field Ambulances

4 x RASC Transport companies

Royal Artillery:

 Field Artillery Regiment: 25-pdr/ 105mm

 Field Artillery Regiment: 25-pdr/ 105mm

 Field Artillery Regiment: 25-pdr/ 105mm

 Anti-tank Regiment

 Lt. Anti-aircraft Regiment:

Royal Engineers:

 Field Squadron

 Field Squadron

 Field Park Squadron

<u>Armoured Brigade:</u>

Armoured Regiment: *HQ Squadron and 3 Squadrons*

Armoured Regiment: *HQ Squadron and 3 Squadrons*

Armoured Regiment: *HQ Squadron and 3 Squadrons*

Motor Battalion: *4 rifle companies*

<u>Motor Infantry Brigade:</u>

Motor Battalion

Motor Battalion

Motor Battalion

Typical Armoured Division April 1943

Divisional Troops:

Divisional Headquarters

Armoured Recce Regiment (type B)

Independent Machine Gun Company

Signals

Workshop REME

2 x Field Ambulances

4 x RASC Transport companies

Royal Artillery:

Field Artillery Regiment: *25-pdr*

Field Artillery Regiment: *Self Propelled 25-pdr*

Anti-tank Regiment

Lt. Anti-aircraft Regiment:

Royal Engineers:

Field Squadron

Field Squadron

Field Park Squadron

Armoured Brigade Group:

Armoured Regiment: *HQ Squadron and 3 x Squadrons*

Armoured Regiment: *HQ Squadron and 3 x Squadrons*

Armoured Regiment: *HQ Squadron and 3 x Squadrons*

Motor Battalion: *4 rifle companies*

Infantry Brigade:

Motor Battalion

Motor Battalion

Motor Battalion

Brigade Support Group (Company)

<u>Typical Armoured Division March 1944</u>

<u>Divisional Troops:</u>

Divisional Headquarters

Armoured Recce Regiment

Signals

Workshop REME

2 x Field Ambulances

4 x RASC Transport companies

Royal Artillery:

Field Artillery Regiment: *25-pdr*

Field Artillery Regiment: *Self Propelled 25-pdr*

Anti-tank Regiment

Lt. Anti-aircraft Regiment:

Royal Engineers:

Field Squadron

Field Squadron

Field Park Squadron

Bridging Troop

<u>Armoured Brigade Group:</u>

Armoured Regiment: *HQ Squadron and 3 x Squadrons*

Armoured Regiment: *HQ Squadron and 3 x Squadrons*

Armoured Regiment: *HQ Squadron and 3 x Squadrons*

Motor Battalion: *4 rifle companies*

<u>Infantry Brigade:</u>

Motor Battalion

Motor Battalion

Motor Battalion

Independent MG Company

The Tanks of the Armoured Divisions:

At the beginning of the war the A9 and A10 tanks represented a new series of British tank that incorporated the concept of cruiser tanks that were lightly armoured and relatively fast compared to the medium tanks of the 1930s. The idea was for many small light tanks to swarm to the enemy like traditional cavalry, using their speed to their advantage and exploiting the gains behind enemy lines. Armour thickness was sacrificed for speed in the Cruiser Tank Series while and the opposite was true in the Infantry Tank Series where speed was sacrificed for heavier armour. The armoured divisions were equipped with Cruiser tanks, using the speed of cruiser tanks for independent action to protect flanks, attacks on an opponent's flanks and rear, pursuit and counter-attack, while the independent armour brigades were mostly equipped with Infantry tanks like the Matilda. However, a number of Infantry tanks also served in the divisions. For example: Matilda Mark I tanks were with the 1st Armoured Division in France 1940 and with them and the 7th Armoured Division in North Africa.

The Cruiser Tank Series was divided into light and heavy where each type equipped a brigade in the original organization of the armoured division. The heavy tanks were more heavily armoured and slightly slower than "light" cruiser tanks.

These tanks were the A13, A13 Mark II, the A13 Mark III "Covenanter" followed in 1940, and the A15 Crusader entered service in 1941.

The M3 Grant arrived in mid-1941 and because of its 75mm gun started to replace the cruiser tanks in the armoured divisions. By the fall of 1942 the M4 Sherman arrived in large supply and joined the M3 Grants, M3 Stuarts, Cruiser Mark IIIs, Cruiser Mark IVs, Crusaders, Matilda and Valentines in the divisions and independent brigades.

Even with the arrived of the reliable M4 Sherman tank the cruiser series wasn't finished. The Cromwell came into service in 1944 and the A34 Comet - a better-armed development of Cromwell - entered service in lesser numbers in late 1944. The Comet tank was a development of the Cromwell, using a modified 17-pounder gun and was fielded in early 1945, by then the firepower and armour protection of cruisers made them indistinguishable from medium tanks. During the war, the development of much more powerful engines and better suspension enabled heavier tanks to approximate the speed of cruisers with the protection of infantry tanks and the concept became obsolete.

The following are the types of tanks that served in the armoured divisions:

Light Tanks:

Cheap and easy to make the light tanks of the British Army were designed to act as cavalry and were lightly armed and armoured. Until the arrival of the M3 they were more armoured cars on tracks than tanks.

Tank, Light, Mark VI:

The sixth version of the light tank that was first designed in 1928 by Vickers. The VI first appeared in 1936. It had a crew of 3, 14mm maximum armour and was armed with only a .50 cal. and a .303 machine guns both in its turret. It weighed 5.2 tons and could reach the speed of 35mph. The VI's main drawback was that it was only armed with two machine guns, which was useless against proper tanks.

The IVC version had no cupola and both machine guns in the turret were replaced with 2 Besa Guns.

The tank was in every major battle that the British fought until 1941, except the Battle of Norway where the ship carrying the tanks was sunk.

These tanks were in the Light Armoured Brigades and were grouped into squadrons of 16 tanks each. The total number of tanks per regiment at this time was 52 Mark VI Light tanks and 12 Daimler Dingo Scout Cars.

After the Mark VIBs and VICs were finally replaced they were used in keep the peace in the Middle East.

M3 Light (Stuart):

The United States' first contribution to the war in North Africa. The 12 ton tank had a 37mm gun, 43mm armour and could reach 35 mph. Since it had been in development for a decade it was mechanically very reliable. However, by the time that it reached the front it was a step behind the German tanks. In North Africa it was said that its thin armour precluded close combat while its small gun demanded it.

Above: the U.S. made M3 Light or as it was known, Stuart tank. It was a big improvement on the other light tanks, but still a step behind the German designs.

Right: Medium Tanks Mark II on exercise in 1939.

Cruiser Tanks:

A series of tanks developed between 1936 and 1939, which was inspired by General Wavell's 1936 visit to the Soviet Army's manoeuvres where he witnessed the performance of the BS series of tanks. The Cruiser series would consider of light, fast moving tanks and support the infantry by striking into the enemy's rear. The name Cruiser comes from naval analogy.

Tank, Cruiser, Mark I (A9):

The A9 was designed in 1934 by Carden as a lighter and cheaper than the expensive Medium Mk III and made by Vickers-Armstrong. It had a small wheel suspension and was the first tank to mount the new 2-pdr gun. A 125 were ordered in 1937. The design became known as General Staff number A9. The tanks was capable of 25 mph (40 km/h) and carried a highly-effective 2-pounder anti-tank gun.

Tank, Cruiser, Mark II (A10):

Originally designed as an infantry tank, but it was quickly discovered that its 30mm armour was insufficient for the role. However, it fit the role of a "heavy cruiser" tank and was put into production in July 1938. It had the same 2-pdr. gun as the A9 and was the first design to be equipped with the Besa machine gun.

Experience during the Battle of France in 1940 revealed the A10's shortcomings, including inadequate armour and a lack of space for the crew. However, it saw useful service in the Western desert and Greece in 1941.

Tank, Cruiser, Mark III (A13 Mark I):

The tank's Nuffield suspension was most effective and performed well in North Africa. The Mk III weighed 31,400 pounds (14.2 t), had a crew of 4, a 340 hp engine which gave a top speed of 30 mph (48 km/h) and was armed with a 2-pounder (40 mm) gun and a machine gun. Production started in 1937.

Tank, Cruiser, Mark IV (A13 Mark II):

Extra armour was added to the A13 Mark I to a max. of 30mm and the tank was modified to allow the turret of the A9 to be mounted. The tank could reach 30 mph (48 km/h). Forty tanks were sent to France in 1940 with the British 1st Armoured Division and most of them were lost in action.

Tank, Cruiser, Mark V (A13 Mark III Covenanter):

The A13 Mark III had heavier armour and production started in 1938 and is considered to be a completely different tank than the A13 Mark I and Mark II. It was designed as a heavy cruiser tank and was known as the Covenanter. The tank entered service in the summer of 1941 with the 1st Armoured Division. However, when the division left the UK to fight in North Africa their Covenanter tanks never did. They were transferred to the 9th Armoured Division still in the UK.

The design had numerous teething problems and despite its speed, low silhouette and dashing appearance, by the time they were worked out the tank was obsolete and could not be upgraded. Its only claim to fame was that of a training tank. The only Covenanter to be destroyed by enemy action was during an air raid in the Canterbury area where the tank was bombed.

Tank, Cruiser, Mark VI (A15 Crusader):

During the early years of World War II, the Crusader was probably the best-known cruiser after it was first used in mid-1941 and used in large numbers in the Western Desert Campaign. Crusader had a reliable Christie suspension. By May 1942 enough tanks were available and shipped to the 6th Royal Tank Regiment who used them in Operation Battleaxe in June 1941 to relieve Torbuk. Even though the Germans respected it for its speed the tank was under-gunned and had the tendency to burst into flames when hit. Later versions of the Crusader was up-gunned with the Mk.III 6-pounder gun.

Tank, Cruiser, Mark VII (A27 Cromwell):

The tank had a Christie suspension in a Meteor engine and a 6-pounder gun before it was replaced by a 75mm gun that could use U.S. ammunition. It was reliable and was popular with its crews. It was first produced in January 1943 and went through eight marks and several variations, including a AOP (fitted with a dummy gun and extra radio equipment) and ARV that had its turret removed and fitted with a crane for recovering damaged tanks while under fire.

Tank, Cruiser, Mark VIII (A30 Challenger):

A 17-pdr gun was mounted on a chassis from a Cromwell tank and built in only limited numbers. It was unpopular with its crews because of the lack of armour and its high profile. Production was slow because the focus was on the Firefly and the Comet instead.

Tank, Cruiser, A34 Comet:

The last of the Cruiser series. The design was based on the Cromwell hull, with extra armour, improved suspension and a wider turret ring to accept a variation of a 17-pdr gun. The tank was first used in March 1945 and is regarded as the best British war-time tank design to see action.

Infantry Tanks:

The Infantry tanks series was based on the experience of WWI where large, well protected, slow moving tanks accompanied the foot soldiers in an assault.

Tank, Infantry, Mark I (Matilda Mark I):

The design was built to price rather than up to a standard because the cost of each tank was to cost no more than 6,000pds. The design had only two men, a driver and a commander/gunner who operated the machine gun in the turret. Its speed was 8 mph (13 km/h). Production started in 1937 and 137 were built, where most of them were sent to France and lost in 1940 because they were inadequate as a tank. The name was based on Matilda the duck because the tank appeared to waddled along.

Tank, Infantry, Mark II (Matilda Mark II):

Realizing that the machine gun was basically useless the tank was designed with a 2-pdr gun in the turret. The Mark II was larger and needed a four man crew. Production started in 1938 and only a few reached France in 1940. However, those who did reach the front gave a good account of themselves where they seemed to be immune to German anti-tank guns. They were impervious to German anti-tank guns until the famed 88mm gun was used in the anti-tank role. The speed was 16 mph (25 km/h)

Tank, Infantry, Mark III (Valentine):

The Valentine was an acronym of its supplier, which was Vickers Armstrong Limited (Engineers) Newcastle-upon-Tyne. The design was meant to be a cheaper version of the Matilda II. It had a

Above: a column of Matilda Mark II tanks follow its commander as he gives hand signals. They were nicknamed The Queen of the Desert.

Above: the rear view of newly manufactured Valentine tanks showing the distinctive engine compartment. Air was taken in over the engine and expelled by fans through the sloping armour.

Top right: a Valentine I being inspected soon after it was built.

Bottom right: a Churchill infantry tank.

2-pdr gun and thin armour. Delivers of the Mark I began in May 1940 and the Director of Armoured Fighting Vehicles, Major General Vyvyan Pope, regarded Valentines as a stop gap and denied their suitability as infantry tanks due to its inferior protection.

In September 1941 the General Staff declared it obsolete. However, even though it failed as an infantry tank, it succeeded as a gun platform as the Archer and Bishop, an observation vehicles, bridge layer, amphibious tank and a tractor.

Tank, Infantry, Mark IV (Churchill):

It was expected in 1939 that the fighting would revert to trench warfare of the WWI so it felt that it was necessary to develop a heavy infantry tank to safely cover no man's land. The Mark I

Above: a Grant tank showing its 75mm gun.

(A22) had a 2-pdr in the turret and a 3" howitzer in the hull, 60mm armour and a 5 man crew.

The Mark II replaced the 75mm gun with a machine gun. The Mark III replaced the 2-pdr. Gun with a 6-pdr. gun and 6 major varieties took place afterwards. The tank was also a base for a wide variety of specialized armour, such as AVREs, bridging tanks, flamethrowers etc.

It was first delivered in June 1941 and first used in action in the Dieppe raid. It was then used in Tunisia where it faired better.

United States Made Medium Tanks:

In June 1940 a British purchasing commission arrived in the U.S. in hopes of having British tanks made for them. The U.S. government was adamant that all U.S. tank facilities were to be used to make U.S. tank designs only, and if the British wanted to buy tanks they would have to buy U.S. designs. At the time the only two designs approaching production were the M3 Light and the M3 Medium. The British ordered both and the M3 Light was the first to be supplied to the British in North Africa.

M3 Medium (Lee/Grant):

The Grant was the British version of the M3 Medium tank, which was rushed into production three weeks after being designed in March 1941.

The British altered the original design by elimanting the cupula at the top and by redesigning the turret to carry the radio, which the U.S. carried in the hull. These modifications became known as the Grant while the original version became known as the Lee.

First deliveries of the Grant started in 1942 and were in action in May 1942 at the Gazala battle. The tank was mechanically reliable and was the first British tank to have a 75mm gun, despite it being in the hull instead of the turret. However, the 75mm gun not being in a turret was a serious disadvantage and once the M4 Sherman came around the M3 was used against the Japanese where it excelled at bunker busting.

M4 Sherman:

The design for the M4 called for a 75mm gun in a turret and with a lower silhouette, which was based on British observations. The lower hull, engine, transmission and running gear were based on the M3 Medium components so that the production lines could be changed from the M3 to the M4 with the least delay.

Production started in February 1942 and the first two Shermans made were for the British army and bore their numbers. The design was reliable, but became seriously outgunned by better German designs during the last few years of the war. To counter this the British rearmed some of their tanks with a 17-pdr gun, calling them the Firefly.

Above: a row of M4 Sherman tanks.

Right: a number of M3 light tanks with a few M4 Shermans.

Royal Armoured Corps:

The Royal Armoured Corps was created in April 1939 and the names of their units came from a variety of sources. The following cavalry designations were used:

Dragoons

Lancers

Hussars

Carabiners

Armoured regiments of the Territorial Army combined their county with Yeomanry for their name. The Royal Tank Regiment numbered its Regular Army tank battalions from 1 to 12 and the Territory Army tank battalions 40 to 51. Royal Armoured Corps battalions were organized by the Corps form 1941 and from converted infantry battalions and were numbered 107 to 163.

Supporting Arms

Royal Artillery:

The Royal Artillery retained its historic title of a `regiment' instead of using battalions. The division had field, anti-tanks and light anti-aircraft regiments as part of its war establishment. The Royal Horse Artillery was a component of the Royal Artillery, but retained their own title and insignia.

The standard gun for a field regiment was the 25-pdr. Gun. The general practice towards the end of the war was to have one field regiment per brigade and if the brigade was armoured then the field regiment was usually self propelled using equipment like the M7 Priest.

The standard anti-tank gun at the beginning of the war was the 2-pdr. Gun, but that quickly became inadequate so it was upgraded to the 6-pdr. This too, by the last year of the war, became inadequate with the newer German tank designs so the 17-prdr. was introduced. There was only one anti-tank regiment per division.

There was also only one light anti-aircraft regiment per division.

The Corps of Royal Engineers:

Once the armoured division's war establishment finally stopped changing the general practice was to have one field squadron (or company) per brigade and in the armoured division this meant that one of the two field squadrons was in halftracks while the other was transported in lorries.

For every division there was one field park squadron (or company) supporting the field companies by supplying and maintaining heavy equipment such as bulldozers and cranes. The field park also carried 80 feet of bridging until the bridging troop was detached from the field park squadron and made independent.

The Royal Corps of Signals:

The branch was responsible for communication and used wireless, telephone, teleprinter and telegraph machines. A battalion size of signallers supported each division and they usually carried the division's number and its designation. These units have not been shown.

Infantry:

There was a very low number of infantry in early armoured divisions. Eventually each armoured division had a brigade of infantry, a motor battalion with the armoured brigade and independent machine gun battalion. Usually each of those battalions kept their regimental system being the `x' battalion of the `x' regiment.

Reconnaissance Corps:

The Reconnaissance Corps was created in January 1941 to be the eyes and ears of the infantry divisions and these were inherited into the mixed divisions. Usually the recce regiment bore the division's number. The regiment operated armoured and scout cars. In an armoured division the general practice was for them to use light tanks and these regiments usually came from the RAC.

The Reconnaissance Corps went through numerous changes and as a result the same unit experienced a number of different name changes during its time in a division. The Reconnaissance Corps was absorbed into the RAC in January 1944.

The Services

The following units are not shown, but were part of the divisions.

Royal Army Service Corps (RASC):

The RASC was responsible for storage, transportation and issue of supplies.

Royal Army Medical Corps (RAMC):

The RAMC was responsible for all medical services.

Royal Army Ordnance Corps (RAOC):

The RAOC procured and issued armament, ammunition, fighting vehicles etc. and prior to the creation of REME, the maintenance and recovery of all equipment.

Royal Electrical and Mechanical Engineers (REME):

REME was formed in 1942 and was responsible for all major vehicle and technical equipment maintenance and repair.

Small Units:

Also part of the division were members of the numerous services from Intelligence Corps to Army Dental Corps.

Numbering:

The following eleven armoured divisions served in World War II and the numbering is not consisted. The 3rd Armoured Division, 4th Armoured Division and 5th Armoured Division were never formed and the 42nd Armoured Division and 79th Armoured Division were converted from infantry divisions, hence the high numbering. Of course, The Guards Armoured Division doesn't fit numerically.

1st Armoured Division

2nd Armoured Division

6th Armoured Division

7th Armoured Division

8th Armoured Division

9th Armoured Division

10th Armoured Division

11th Armoured Division

42nd Armoured Division

79th Armoured Division

Guards Armoured Division

1st Armoured Division

The 1st Armoured Division was a regular division in September 1939 after first forming as the Mobile Division in 1937. It went to France on May 22/23rd 1940 as part of the BEF where it lost most of its tanks. Upon return its six armoured regiments were re-equipped with the ill fated Covenanter tanks. However, before the division left the UK it transferred all of these tanks to the 9th Armoured Division and re-equipped with light and cruiser tanks in North Africa.

In November 1940 it exchanged its experienced, but battered 3rd Armoured Brigade for the inexperienced 22nd Armoured Brigade of the 2nd Armoured Division. For the next two years the 1st Armoured Division participated in the battles of Gazala, Mersa, Matruh, the Defense of the Alamein Line, El Alamein, Tebaga Gap, Wadi Akarit, El Kourzia and Tunis. Later in 1944 it fought in the battle of Coriano, and because of heavy losses, by October it was finished as a division mainly because of the lack of replacements to replace the severe casualties that the division sustained.

In August 1944 the 627th Field Squadron, RE and the 631st Field Park Squadron, RE replaced the 7th Field Squadron, RE and 1st Field Park Squadron, RE. They, the 4th Hussars and the Royal Artillery left the division in September. The 2nd Armoured Brigade and 18th Infantry Brigade left in November after ceasing operations in October. The 2nd Armoured Brigade became an independent Armoured Brigade while the 18th was broken up for replacements in other divisions. The division disbanded officially on January 11th, 1945.

The divisional sign was a charging rhino and it's commanding officers were: Major Generals Roger Evans, Willoughby Norrie, Herbert Lumsden, Frank Messervy, Raymond Briggs, Alexander Galloway and Richard Hull.

1st Armoured Division 1939

Divisional Troops

2nd Light Armoured Brigade:

    Queen's Bays Armoured Regiment

    9th Lancers Armoured Regiment

    10th Hussars Armoured Regiment

1st Heavy Armoured Brigade:

    2nd Royal Tank Regiment

    3rd Royal Tank Regiment

    5th Royal Tank Regiment

1st Support Group:

    1st Battalion, the Rifle Brigade

    2nd Battalion, Kings Royal Rifle Corps

    Royal Artillery:

        1st Regiment Royal Horse Artillery

        2nd Regiment Royal Horse Artillery

        60th Anti-tank Regiment, RA: *2 pounder guns*

1st Armoured Division 1940

Divisional Troops

12th Lancers: *Morris CS9 armoured cars*

Royal Engineers:

1st Field Squadron, RE

7th Field Squadron, RE

1st Field Park Troop, RE

2nd Armoured Brigade:

Queen's Bays Armoured Regiment: *3 Cruiser Sqn, 1 Lt. Tank Sqn.*

9th Lancers Armoured Regiment: *3 Cruiser Sqn., 1 Lt. Tank Sqn.*

10th Hussars Armoured Regiment: *3 Cruiser Sqn., 1 Lt. Tank Sqn.*

1st Battalion, Kings Royal Rifle Corps

3rd Armoured Brigade:

2nd Royal Tank Regiment: *3 Cruiser Sqn., 1 Lt. Tank Sqn.*

3rd Royal Tank Regiment: *3 Cruiser Sqn., 1 Lt. Tank Sqn.*

5th Royal Tank Regiment: *3 Cruiser Sqn., 1 Lt. Tank Sqn.*

1st Support Group:

4th Battalion, Borders

Royal Artillery:

11th Regiment Royal Horse Artillery, RA

101st Light Anti-aircraft/Anti-tank Regiment, RA

1st Armoured Division November 1940

Divisional Troops

12th Lancers: *Beaverettes armoured cars*

Royal Engineers:

    1st Field Squadron, RE

    7th Field Squadron, RE

    1st Field Park Squadron, RE

2nd Armoured Brigade:

Queen's Bays Armoured Regiment: *3 Cruiser Sqn, 1 Lt. Tank Sqn.*

9th Lancers Armoured Regiment: *3 Cruiser Sqn., 1 Lt. Tank Sqn.*

10th Hussars Armoured Regiment: *3 Cruiser Sqn., 1 Lt. Tank Sqn.*

1st Battalion, Kings Royal Rifle Corps

22nd Armoured Brigade:

2nd Royal Gloucestershire Hussars: *Crusaders*

3rd County of London Yeomanry: *Crusaders*

4th Country of London Yeomanry: *Crusaders*

2nd Battalion, Kings Royal Rifle Corps

1st Support Group:

4th Battalion, Borders

Royal Artillery:

    11th Regiment Royal Horse Artillery

    76th Anti-tank Regiment, RA

    61st Light Anti-aircraft Regiment, RA

1st Armoured Division February 1942

Divisional Troops

    12th Lancers: *Humber armoured cars*

    Royal Engineers:

        1st Field Park Squadron, RE

2nd Armoured Brigade:

    Queen's Bays Armoured Regiment: *A: Crusader B: Crusader C: Grant*

    9th Lancers Armoured Regiment: *A: Crusader B: Grant C: Crusader*

    10th Hussars Armoured Regiment: *A: Crusader B: Crusader C: Grant*

    1st Battalion, Kings Royal Rifle Corps

    11th Regiment Royal Horse Artillery

    88th Light Anti-aircraft Battery, RA

200th Guards Brigade (201st Guards Motor Brigade from May 42)

    3rd Battalion, Coldstream Guards

    2nd Battalion, Scots Guards

    9th Battalion, the Rifle Brigade

    1st Field Squadron, RE

1st Support Group:

    9th Battalion, Foresters (1941 only)

    2nd Battalion, Kings Royal Rifle Corps

    7th Field Squadron, RE

    Royal Artillery:

        2nd Regiment Royal Horse Artillery

        76th Anti-tank Regiment, RA

        44th Light Anti-aircraft Battery, RA

1st Armoured Division Late 1942

Divisional Troops:

12th Lancers: *Humber armoured cars*

Royal Artillery:

2nd Regiment Royal Horse Artillery

4th Regiment Royal Horse Artillery

11th Regiment Royal Horse Artillery

76th Anti-tank Regiment , RA

42nd Light Anti-aircraft Regiment, RA

Royal Engineers:

1st Field Squadron, RE

7th Field Squadron, RE

1st Field Park Squadron, RE

2nd Armoured Brigade:

Queen's Bays Armoured Regiment: *A: Crusaders B+C: Shermans*

9th Lancers Armoured Regiment: *A: Crusaders B+C: Shermans*

10th Hussars Armoured Regiment: *A+C: Shermans B: Crusaders*

1st Battalion, Kings Royal Rifle Corps

7th Motor Brigade:

1st Battalion, Buffs (Royal East Kent Regiment)

14th Battalion, Foresters

9th Battalion, Kings Own Yorkshire Light Infantry

1st Armoured Division 1943

Divisional Troops:

12th Lancers: *Humber armoured cars*

Royal Artillery:

2nd Regiment Royal Horse Artillery

4th Regiment Royal Horse Artillery (to November)

11th Regiment Royal Horse Artillery

76th Anti-tank Regiment, RA

42nd Light Anti-aircraft Regiment, RA

Royal Engineers:

1st Field Squadron, RE

7th Field Squadron, RE

1st Field Park Squadron, RE

27th Bridging Troop, RE (from November)

2nd Armoured Brigade:

Queen's Bays Armoured Regiment:

9th Lancers Armoured Regiment

10th Hussars Armoured Regiment

1st (Motor) Battalion, Kings Royal Rifle Corps (from June)

18th Infantry Brigade:

1st Battalion, Buffs (Royal East Kent Regiment)

14th Battalion, Foresters

9th Battalion, Kings Own Yorkshire Light Infantry

1st Armoured Division 1944

Divisional Troops:

12th Lancers (to April): *Humber armoured cars*

4th Hussars (from May)

Royal Artillery:

2nd Regiment Royal Horse Artillery

11th Regiment Royal Horse Artillery

76th Anti-tank Regiment, RA

42nd Light Anti-aircraft Regiment, RA

Royal Engineers:

1st Field Squadron, RE

7th Field Squadron, RE

1st Field Park Squadron, RE

27th Bridging Troop, RE

2nd Armoured Brigade:

Queen's Bays Armoured Regiment

9th Lancers Armoured Regiment

10th Hussars Armoured Regiment

1st (Motor) Battalion, Kings Royal Rifle Corps

18th Infantry Brigade:

1st Battalion, Buffs (Royal East Kent Regiment)

14th Battalion, Foresters

9th Battalion, Kings Own Yorkshire Light Infantry

2nd Armoured Division

The division began forming in January 1940 in the UK and arrived in the Middle East January 1941 without one of its Armoured Brigades (who became independent) and motor battalions. The division exchanged its 22nd Armoured Brigade for the more experienced 3rd Armoured Brigade from the 1st Armoured Division, which needed to be rebuilt. The British thought that Rommel wouldn't be able to attack until May so they focused on rebuilding the under strength division and in particular, the battered 3rd Armoured Brigade who had approximately half of its tanks being captured Italian tanks because of the lack of reserve tanks. The other half was the newly arrived 5th Royal Tank Regiment.

The British were wrong and Rommel attacked on March 24th. The weakened division fought its one and only battle in Libya where its divisional headquarters, armoured brigade and support group were captured by Rommel in April 1941. It's General Officer Commanding, Major General Gambier-Parry, was also captured. The division more or less ceased to exist so what was left was disbanded in May, never having its battle insignia of a plumed knight's helmet authorized.

2nd Armoured Division Early 1940

Divisional Troops

1st Light Armoured Brigade:

    Kings Dragoon Guards: *Mark VI Light Tanks*

    3rd Hussars: *Mark VI Light Tanks*

    4th Hussars: *Mark VI Light Tanks*

22nd Heavy Armoured Brigade:

    2nd Royal Gloucestershire Hussars

    3rd County of London Yeomanry

    4th County of London Yeomanry

2nd Support Group:

    1st Battalion, Rangers

    1st Battalion, Tower Hamlets Rifles

    Royal Artillery:

        2nd Regiment Royal Horse Artillery

        12th Regiment Royal Horse Artillery

        102nd Light Anti-aircraft/Anti-tank Regiment, RA

    Royal Engineers:

        3rd Field Squadron, RE

        142nd Field Park Squadron, RE

2nd Armoured Division April 1940

Divisional Troops

1st Armoured Brigade:

>   King's Dragoon Guards

>   3rd Hussars

>   4th Hussars

22nd Armoured Brigade:

>   2nd Royal Gloucestershire Hussars

>   3rd County of London Yeomanry

>   4th Country of London Yeomanry

2nd Support Group:

>   1st Battalion, Rangers

>   1st Battalion, Tower Hamlets Rifles

>   Royal Artillery:

>>   2nd Regiment Royal Horse Artillery

>>   12th Regiment Royal Horse Artillery

>>   102nd Light Anti-aircraft/Anti-tank Regiment, RA

>   Royal Engineers:

>>   3rd Field Squadron, RE

>>   142nd Field Park Squadron, RE

2nd Armoured Division 1941

Divisional Troops

King's Dragoon Guards (from Feb.): *Mk. VI Light tanks*

Royal Engineers:

>3rd Field Squadron, RE

>142nd Field Park Squadron, RE

1st Armoured Brigade: (to Feb. only)

>Kings Dragoon Guards

>4th Hussars

>3rd Royal Tank Regiment

3rd Armoured Brigade:

>3rd Hussars: *captured M13/40 tanks**

>5th Royal Tank Regiment: *2xA9C and 14xA-13 tanks*

>6th Royal Tank Regiment: *captured M13/40 tanks***

2nd Support Group:

>1st Battalion, Rangers

>1st Battalion, Tower Hamlets Rifles

>Royal Artillery:

>>2nd Regiment Royal Horse Artillery

>>104th Regiment Royal Horse Artillery

>>102nd Light Anti-aircraft/Anti-tank Regiment, RA (to Feb.)

>>15th Light Anti-aircraft Regiment, RA (from Feb.)

---

* the captured M13/40 had sandbags on the hull, which counted as an extra cm of improvised armour. RHQ was 4x Vickers VIB, A Sqn.: 11xVickers VIB, B Sqn.: 12xM13/40 and C Sqn.: 11X Vickers VIB.

** A Sqn.: 16xM13/40, B Sqn.: 12xVickers VIB and C Sqn.: 16xM13/40

6th Armoured Division

The division formed in September 1940 and stayed in the UK until 1942. The armoured regiments were initially supplied with Matilda and Valentine tanks. These were replaced with Crusader tanks. The division was part of Operation Torch in November 1942.

From the wide open spaces of the desert the division next fought in the mountains of Italy supporting the infantry. The division fought in Italy from March 1944 and finished the war in Austria. Its battles were: Bou Arada, Fondouk, El Kourzia, Tunis, Liri Valley, Arezzo, Florence, Gothic Line and Aregentia Gap.

The division's first General Officer Commanding was Major General John Crochen and after a dozen other commanders its last General Officer Commanding was Major General Horatius Murray.

It's divisional insignia was the mailed fist.

6th Armoured Division 1940

Divisional Troops

1st Derbyshire Yeomanry: *armoured cars*

Royal Engineers:

    5th Field Squadron, RE

    8th Field Squadron, RE

    144th Field Park Squadron, RE

20th Armoured Brigade:

1st Royal Gloucestershire Hussars: *Crusader and Valentines*

1st Northamptonshire Yeomanry: *Crusader and Valentines*

2nd Northamptonshire Yeomanry: *Crusader and Valentines*

2nd Battalion, Rangers Regiment

26th Armoured Brigade:

16th/5th Lancers: *Crusader and Valentines*

17th/21st Lancers: *Crusader and Valentines*

2nd Lothian and Border Horse: *Crusader and Valentines*

2nd Battalion, Tower Hamlets Rifles

6th Support Group:

Royal Artillery:

    12th Regiment Royal Horse Artillery

    72nd Anti-tank Regiment, RA

6th Armoured Division 1941

<u>Divisional Troops</u>

1st Derbyshire Yeomanry: *armoured cars*

Royal Engineers:

5th Field Squadron, RE

8th Field Squadron, RE

144th Field Park Squadron, RE

<u>20th Armoured Brigade:</u>

1st Royal Gloucestershire Hussars: *Crusader and Valentines*

1st Northamptonshire Yeomanry: *Crusader and Valentines*

2nd Northamptonshire Yeomanry: *Crusader and Valentines*

10th Battalion, Kings Royal Rifle Corps

<u>26th Armoured Brigade:</u>

16th/5th Lancers: *Crusader and Valentines*

17th/21st Lancers: *Crusader and Valentines*

2nd Lothian and Border Horse: *Crusader and Valentines*

10th Battalion, the Rifle Brigade

<u>6th Support Group:</u>

9th Queen's Own Rifles (West Kent Regiment)

Royal Artillery:

12th Regiment Royal Horse Artillery

72nd Anti-tank Regiment, RA

51st Light Anti-aircraft Regiment, RA

6th Armoured Division June 1942

Divisional Troops

1st Derbyshire Yeomanry: *armoured cars*

Royal Artillery:

12th Regiment Royal Horse Artillery

152nd Field Regiment, RA

72nd Anti-tank Regiment, RA

51st Light Anti-aircraft Regiment, RA

Royal Engineers:

5th Field Squadron, RE

8th Field Squadron, RE

144th Field Park Squadron, RE

26th Armoured Brigade:

16th/5th Lancers: *Crusaders and Valentines*

17th/21st Lancers: *Crusaders and Valentines*

2nd Lothian and Border Horse: *Crusaders and Valentines*

10th Battalion, the Rifle Brigade

38th (Irish) Infantry Brigade:

2nd Battalion, London Irish Rifles

1st Battalion, Royal Irish Fusiliers

6th Battalion, Royal Inniskilling Fusiliers

6th Armoured Division March 1943

Divisional Troops

1st Derbyshire Yeomanry: *armoured cars*

Royal Artillery:

12th Regiment Royal Horse Artillery

152nd Field Regiment, RA

72nd Anti-tank Regiment, RA

51st Light Anti-aircraft Regiment, RA

Royal Engineers:

5th Field Squadron, RE

8th Field Squadron, RE

144th Field Park Squadron, RE

26th Armoured Brigade:

16th/5th Lancers: *Sherman tanks*

17th/21st Lancers: *Sherman tanks*

2nd Lothian and Border Horse: *Sherman tanks*

10th Battalion, the Rifle Brigade

1st Infantry Brigade (Guards):

3rd Battalion, Grenadier Guards

2nd Battalion, Coldstream Guards

3rd Battalion, Welsh Guards

6th Armoured Division May 1944

Divisional Troops

1st Derbyshire Yeomanry: *armoured cars*

Royal Artillery:

12th Regiment Royal Horse Artillery

152nd Field Regiment, RA

72nd Anti-tank Regiment, RA

51st Light Anti-aircraft Regiment, RA

Royal Engineers:

5th Field Squadron, RE

8th Field Squadron, RE

144th Field Park Squadron, RE

6th Bridging Troop, RE

26th Armoured Brigade:

16th/5th Lancers: *Sherman tanks*

17th/21st Lancers: *Sherman tanks*

2nd Lothian and Border Horse: *Sherman tanks*

61st Infantry Brigade:

2nd Battalion, the Rifle Brigade

7th Battalion, the Rifle Brigade

10th Battalion, the Rifle Brigade

7th Armoured Division

The regular division in September 1939 that was `Armoured Division (Egypt)' under General Hobart and was one of only two armoured divisions in existence at the beginning of the war. Actually to call it an armoured division at this time would be a stretch because it was more or less a collection of a headquarters, a few divisional troops and two brigades of tanks. There wasn't any artillery or engineers yet.

It became the 7th Armoured Division in February 1940. It was nicknamed, `the Desert Rats' after their divisional sign of a rat and the fact that they started the war in the desert.

The division fought in North Africa, Italy and Northwest Europe and its battles were: Sidi Barami, Bardia, the Capture of Tobruk, Beda Fomm, Tobruk, Gazala, Alamein Line, Alam El Halfia, El Alamein, Medenine, Mareth, Akarit, Enfidaville, Tunis, Salerno, Naples, Volurno Crossing, Bourgeubus Ridge, Neder Rijn and the Rhine.

During its time in North Africa the division had three armoured/tanks brigades, but lost the tank brigade before the armoured divisions in North Africa were reorganized by General Auinleck after Operation Crusader.

Armoured Division (Egypt) 1939

Light Armoured Brigade (Egypt):

      7th Hussars: *52 Mark III and Mark IV Light tanks*

      8th King's R. Irish Hussars: *52 Mark III and Mark IV Light tanks*

      11th Hussars (Prince Albert's Own): *obsolete armoured cars*

Heavy Armoured Brigade (Egypt):

      1st Royal Tank Regiment

      6th Royal Tank Regiment

7th Armoured Division February 1940

7th Light Armoured Brigade:

7th Hussars: *52 Mark III and Mark IV Light tanks*

8th Kings R. Irish Hussars: *52 Mark III and Mark IV Light tanks*

11th Hussars: (Prince Albert's Own): *armoured cars*

4th Heavy Armoured Brigade:

1st Royal Tank Regiment

2nd Royal Tank Regiment: *A9, A10 and A13*

6th Royal Tank Regiment

7th Support Group:

1st Battalion, Kings Royal Rifle Corps

2nd Battalion, the Rifle Brigade

Royal Artillery:

   3rd Regiment Royal Horse Artillery

   4th Regiment Royal Horse Artillery

   60th Anti-tank Regiment, RA

7th Armoured Division March 1941

Divisional Troops

    11th Hussars: (Prince Albert's Own): *armoured cars*

    Royal Engineers:

        4th Field Squadron, RE

        143rd Field Park Squadron, RE

7th Armoured Brigade:

    6th Royal Tank Regiment: *Crusaders from May*

    8th King's Royal Irish Hussars

    1st Royal Tank Regiment

4th Armoured Brigade:

    4th Royal Tank Regiment

    2nd Royal Tank Regiment

    7th Hussars: *Crusaders*

1st Army Tank Brigade: (August to November only)

    8th Royal Tank Regiment

    42nd Royal Tank Regiment

    44th Royal Tank Regiment

7th Support Group:

    1st Battalion, Kings Royal Rifle Corps

    2nd Battalion, the Rifle Brigade

    Royal Artillery:

        3rd Regiment Royal Horse Artillery

        4th Regiment Royal Horse Artillery

        60th Anti-tank Regiment, RA

        1st Light Anti-aircraft Regiment, RA

        Battery/38th Light Anti-aircraft Regiment, RA (April and May)

7th Armoured Division March 1942

Divisional Troops

11th Hussars: (Prince Albert's Own): *armoured cars*

Royal Artillery:

3rd Regiment Royal Horse Artillery

60th Anti-tank Regiment, RA

1st Light Anti-aircraft Regiment, RA

Royal Engineers:

143rd Field Park Squadron, RE

4th Armoured Brigade:

3rd Royal Tank Regiment

8th King's Royal Irish Hussars: *M3 Stuart*

5th Royal Tank Regiment

7th Motor Brigade:

1st Battalion, Kings Royal Rifle Corps

2nd Battalion, the Rifle Brigade

9th Battalion., Kings Royal Rifle Corps

4th Regiment Royal Horse Artillery

4th Field Squadron, RE

7th Armoured Division July 1942

Divisional Troops

    11th Hussars: (Prince Albert's Own): *armoured cars*

    Royal Artillery:

        3rd Regiment Royal Horse Artillery

        4th Regiment Royal Horse Artillery

        60th Anti-tank Regiment, RA

        1st Light Anti-aircraft Regiment, RA

    Royal Engineers:

        4th Field Squadron, RE

        143rd Field Park Squadron, RE

22nd Armoured Brigade:

    2nd Royal Gloucestershire Hussars

    3rd County of London Yeomanry: *Grants*

    4th County of London Yeomanry: *Grants*

7th Motor Brigade:

    1st Battalion, Buffs (Royal East Kent Regiment)

    9th Battalion., Kings Own Yorkshire Light Infantry

    14th Battalion, Foresters

7th Armoured Division November 1942

Divisional Troops

11th Hussars: (Prince Albert's Own): *armoured cars*

Royal Artillery:

3rd Regiment Royal Horse Artillery

4th Regiment Royal Horse Artillery

60th Anti-tank Regiment, RA

1st Light Anti-aircraft Regiment, RA

Royal Engineers:

4th Field Squadron, RE

21st Field Squadron, RE

143rd Field Park Squadron, RE

22nd Armoured Brigade:

1st Royal Tank Regiment

5th Royal Tank Regiment

4th County of London Yeomanry

1st Battalion, the Rifle Brigade

131st Infantry Brigade:

1/5th Battalion, Queens Royal Regiment

1/6th Battalion, Queens Royal Regiment

1/7th Battalion, Queens Royal Regiment

7th Armoured Division December 1944

Divisional Troops

8th King's Royal Irish Hussars: *M5 Stuarts*

Royal Artillery:

3rd Regiment Royal Horse Artillery

4th Regiment Royal Horse Artillery

60th Anti-tank Regiment, RA

1st Light Anti-aircraft Regiment, RA

Royal Engineers:

4th Field Squadron, RE

621st Field Squadron, RE

143rd Field Park Squadron, RE

22nd Armoured Brigade:

1st Royal Tank Regiment

5th Royal Tank Regiment

5th Royal Inniskilling Dragoon Guards: *Shermans*

1st Battalion, the Rifle Brigade

131st Infantry Brigade:

1/5th Battalion, Queens Royal Regiment

9th Battalion, Durham Light Infantry Regiment

2nd Battalion, Devonshire Regiment

8th Armoured Division

The division started to form in the United Kingdom in November 1940 and began to leave for Egypt in May 1942. Upon arrival it was ordered to exchange one of its armoured brigades for an infantry brigade and dismantled the 8th Support Group to reorganize to the new war establishment. Its 23rd Armoured Brigade Group help defend the Alamein Line.

The 24th Armoured Brigade reorganized as a brigade group and the division never received a lorried infantry brigade to replace the departed 23rd Armoured Brigade. As a result the 8th Armoured Division never fought as a division.

The division headquarters formed Hammerforce from October to November 1942, which consisted of units mostly from the 1st Armoured Division and most of the 8th Armoured Division's Royal Artillery.

Major General Charles Gairdner was its last General Officer Commanding.

On January 1st 1943 the division disbanded, but the name lived on for the purpose of military deception.

The division's insignia was a green GO.

8th Armoured Division November 1940

Divisional Troops

2nd Derbyshire Yeomanry: *armoured cars*

Royal Engineers:

6th Field Squadron, RE

145th Field Park Squadron, RE

23rd Armoured Brigade:

40th Royal Tank Regiment: *Very few Matilda II and Valentines*

46th Royal Tank Regiment: *Very few Matilda II and Valentines*

50th Royal Tank Regiment: *Very few Matilda II and Valentines*

1st Battalion., London Rifle Brigade

24th Armoured Brigade:

41st Royal Tank Regiment: *Very few Matilda II and Valentines*

45th Royal Tank Regiment: *Very few Matilda II and Valentines*

47th Royal Tank Regiment: *Very few Matilda II and Valentines*

1st Battalion., Queen Westminsters

8th Support Group:

14th Battalion, Foresters

Royal Artillery:

5th Regiment Royal Horse Artillery

73rd Anti-tank Regiment, RA

8th Armoured Division 1941

Divisional Troops

2nd Derbyshire Yeomanry: *armoured cars*

Royal Engineers:

6th Field Squadron, RE

9th Field Squadron, RE

145th Field Park Squadron, RE

23rd Armoured Brigade:

40th Royal Tank Regiment: *Matilda II and Valentines*

46th Royal Tank Regiment: *Matilda II and Valentines*

50th Royal Tank Regiment: *Matilda II and Valentines*

7th Battalion., the Rifle Brigade

24th Armoured Brigade:

41st Royal Tank Regiment: *Matilda II and Valentines*

45th Royal Tank Regiment: *Matilda II and Valentines*

47th Royal Tank Regiment: *Matilda II and Valentines*

1st Battalion., Queen Westministers

8th Support Group:

14th Battalion, Foresters

Royal Artillery:

5th Regiment Royal Horse Artillery

73rd Anti-tank Regiment, RA

56th Light Anti-aircraft Regiment, RA

8th Armoured Division November 1942

Divisional Troops

2nd Derbyshire Yeomanry: *armoured cars*

Royal Artillery:

5th Regiment Royal Horse Artillery

146th Field Regiment, RA

73rd Anti-tank Regiment, RA

56th Light Anti-aircraft Regiment, RA

Royal Engineers:

6th Field Squadron, RE

9th Field Squadron, RE

145th Field Park Squadron, RE

24th Armoured Brigade:

41st Royal Tank Regiment: *Crusader / Grants / Shermans*

45th Royal Tank Regiment: *Crusader / Grants / Shermans*

47th Royal Tank Regiment: *Crusader / Grants / Shermans*

11th Battalion, King's Royal Rifle Corps

B/73rd Anti-tank Regiment, RA

116th Light AA Battery, RA

Troop/6th Field Squadron, RE

9th Armoured Division

In December 1940 the division formed in the United Kingdom and never left. It was used primarily for training and its 27th Armoured Brigade was used for experiments with specialized armour until it left in June 1942 where it became part of the 79th Armoured Division when it formed in August 1942. All three of its armoured regiments left in the summer of 1944 to join other brigades. The division was disbanded in July 1944.

The division's insignia was the face of a panda.

The 9th Armoured Division's first commander was Major General Brocas Burrows and he was replaced by Major General Brian Horrocks in March 1942. Major General D'Arcy took over in August 1942.

9th Armoured Division 1941

Divisional Troops

Inns of Court Regiment: *Humber armoured cars*

Royal Engineers:

10th Field Squadron, RE

11th Field Squadron, RE

146th Field Park Squadron, RE

27th Armoured Brigade:

4th/7th Dragoon Guards

13th/18th Hussars: *MK. VI Light tanks to August then Covenanters*

1st East Riding Yeomanry

1st Battalion, Queen Victoria Rifles

28th Armoured Brigade:

5th Royal Innisskilling Dragoon Guards

15th/19th Hussars: *Covenanters*

1st Fife and Forfar Yeomanry

2nd Battalion, Queen Victoria Rifles (Jan. only)

8th Battalion, Kings Royal Rifle Corps

9th Support Group:

11th Battalion, Worcestershire Regiment

Royal Artillery:

6th Regiment Royal Horse Artillery

74th Anti-tank Regiment, RA

54th Light Anti-aircraft Regiment, RA

9th Armoured Division July 1942

Divisional Troops

Inns of Court Regiment: *Humber armoured cars*

Royal Artillery:

6th Regiment Royal Horse Artillery

141st Field Regiment, RA

74th Anti-tank Regiment, RA

54th Light Anti-aircraft Regiment, RA

Royal Engineers:

10th Field Squadron, RE

11th Field Squadron, RE

146th Field Park Squadron, RE

28th Armoured Brigade:

5th Battalion, Royal Inniskilling Dragoon Guards

15th/19th Hussars

1st Fife and Forfar Yeomanry

8th Battalion, Kings Royal Rifle Corps

7th Infantry Brigade:

2nd Battalion, South Wales Borderers

6th Battalion, Royal Sussex Regiment

2/6th Battalion, East Surrey Regiment

9th Armoured Division November 1943

Divisional Troops

1st Royal Gloucestershire Hussars

Royal Artillery:

6th Regiment Royal Horse Artillery

141st Field Regiment, RA

74th Anti-tank Regiment, RA

54th Light Anti-aircraft Regiment, RA

Royal Engineers:

10th Field Squadron, RE

611th Field Squadron, RE

146th Field Park Squadron, RE

9th Bridging Troop, RE

28th Armoured Brigade:

5th Battalion, Royal Inniskilling Dragoon Guards

15th/19th Hussars

1st Fife and Forfar Yeomanry

8th Battalion, Kings Royal Rifle Corps

7th Infantry Brigade:

2nd Battalion, South Wales Borderers

6th Battalion, Royal Sussex Regiment

2/6th Battalion, East Surrey Regiment

10th Armoured Division

The division formed in Palestine from the disbanded 1st Cavalry Division. It relocated to Egypt and fought in the battles of Alam el Halfa and El Alamein before it went back to Palestine. What was left of the division returned to Egypt and was disbanded in June 1944.

The division's General Officer Commanding were: Major General J. Clark, Major General A. Gatehouse, Major General C. Norman and Major General J. Birks.

The division's insignia was a red fox's mask on a yellow disk.

10th Armoured Division 1941

Divisional Troops

1st Household Cavalry Regiment: *armoured cars*

Royal Engineers:

2nd Field Squadron, RE

3rd Field Squadron, RE

141st Field Park Squadron, RE

8th Armoured Brigade:

Royal Scots Greys

Staffordshire Yeomanry

Notts (Sherwood Rangers) Yeomanry

9th Armoured Brigade:

Yorkshire Hussars

Royal Wiltshire Yeomanry

Warwickshire Yeomanry

10th Armoured Division March 1942

Divisional Troops

1st Household Cavalry Regiment: *armoured cars*

Royal Engineers:

2nd Field Squadron, RE

3rd Field Squadron, RE

141st Field Park Squadron, RE

8th Armoured Brigade:

Royal Scots Greys: *Crusaders/ Grants/ Shermans*

Staffordshire Yeomanry: *Crusaders/ Grants/ Shermans*

Notts (Sherwood Rangers) Yeomanry: *Crusaders/Grants/Shermans*

9th Armoured Brigade:

Yorkshire Hussars: *Crusaders/ Grants/ Shermans*

Royal Wiltshire Yeomanry: *Crusaders/ Grants/ Shermans*

Warwickshire Yeomanry: *Crusaders/ Grants/ Shermans*

10th Indian Motor Brigade Group:

1st Battalion, Argyll and Sutherland Highlanders

1/1st Battalion, Punjab Regiment

1/2nd Battalion, Punjab Regiment

3/8th Battalion, Punjab Regiment

The 10th was replaced in June by:

161st Indian Motor Brigade Group:

1st Battalion, Duke of Cornwalls Light Infantry

4/10th Battalion, Baluch Regiment

3/8th Battalion, Royal Garwhal Rifles

2/4th Battalion, Ghurkha Rifles

10th Armoured Division September 1942

Divisional Troops

1st Household Cavalry Regiment: *armoured cars*

Royal Artillery:

1st Regiment, RHA

Royal Engineers:

2nd Field Squadron, RE

3rd Field Squadron, RE

141st Field Park Squadron, RE

8th Armoured Brigade:

Staffordshire Yeomanry: *Crusaders/ Grants/ Shermans*

Notts (Sherwood Rangers) Yeomanry: *Crusaders/Grants/Shermans*

3rd Royal Tank Regiment: *Crusaders/ Grants/ Shermans*

1st Battalion, Buffs (Royal East Kent Regiment)

9th Armoured Brigade:

Yorkshire Hussars: *Crusaders/ Grants/ Shermans*

Royal Wiltshire Yeomanry: *Crusaders/ Grants/ Shermans*

Warwickshire Yeomanry: *Crusaders/ Grants/ Shermans*

7th Motor Brigade:

2nd Battalion, Royal Rifle Corps

2nd Battalion, the Rifle Brigade

7th Battalion, the Rifle Brigade

10th Armoured Division November 1942

Divisional Troops

 1st The Royal Dragoons: *armoured cars*

 Royal Artillery:

  1st Regiment, RHA

  104th Regiment, RHA

  98th Field Regiment, RA

  84th Anti-tank Regiment, RA

  53rd Light Anti-aircraft Regiment, RA

 Royal Engineers:

  2nd Field Squadron, RE

  3rd Field Squadron, RE

  141st Field Park Squadron, RE

8th Armoured Brigade:

 Staffordshire Yeomanry: *Crusaders/ Grants/ Shermans*

 3rd Royal Tank Regiment: *Crusaders/ Grants/ Shermans*

 1st Battalion, Buffs (Royal East Kent Regiment)

9th Armoured Brigade:

 Royal Wiltshire Yeomanry: *Crusaders/ Grants/ Shermans*

 Warwickshire Yeomanry: *Crusaders/ Grants/ Shermans*

 3rd King's Own Hussars: *Crusaders/ Grants/ Shermans*

 11th Battalion, Kings Royal Rifle Corps

133rd Lorried Infantry Brigade:

 4th Battalion, Buffs (Royal East Kent Regiment)

 2nd Battalion, Royal Sussex Regiment

 4th Battalion, Royal Sussex Regiment

 5th Battalion, Royal Sussex Regiment

10th Armoured Division February 1943

Divisional Troops

   1st Household Cavalry Regiment: *armoured cars*

   Royal Artillery:

   1st Regiment, RHA

   104th Regiment, RHA

   84th Anti-tank Regiment, RA

   53rd Light Anti-aircraft Regiment, RA

   Royal Engineers:

   2nd Field Squadron, RE

   3rd Field Squadron, RE

   141st Field Park Squadron, RE

9th Armoured Brigade:

   Royal Wiltshire Yeomanry

   Warwickshire Yeomanry

   3rd Kings Own Hussars

   11th Battalion, Kings Royal Rifle Corps

201st Guards Motor Brigade:

   3rd Battalion, Coldstream Guards

   6th Battalion, Grenadier Guards

   2nd Battalion, Scots Guards

10th Armoured Division April 1944

Divisional Troops

7th Hussars

Royal Artillery:

    1st Regiment, RHA

    104th Regiment, RHA

    84th Anti-tank Regiment, RA

    101st Light Anti-aircraft Regiment, RA

Royal Engineers:

    3rd Field Squadron, RE

    622nd Field Squadron, RE

    141st Field Park Squadron, RE

    6th Bridging Troop, RE

7th Armoured Brigade:

2nd Royal Tank Regiment

6th Royal Tank Regiment

8th Royal Tank Regiment

2nd Battalion, Kings Royal Rifle Corps

10th Armoured Division June 1944

Divisional Troops:

23rd Armoured Brigade:

    40th Royal Tank Regiment

    46th Royal Tank Regiment

    50th Royal Tank Regiment

    1st Battalion, Kings Royal Rifle Corps

11th Armoured Division

The division formed in the United Kingdom in March 1941 and at the time of formation its General Commanding Officer was Major General P.C.S. Hobart who wrote of the division's recruits, "High quality. Mostly 30-40 years of age." and *They are the most diverse assortment...the Butler to Lord X standing next to a Glasgow shop assistant on one side and to a Belfast butcher on the other.*"

The division was equipped with 2-pdr Valentine tanks at first and then 6-pdr Crusader tanks appeared in the summer of 1942. General Hobart left in September 1943 for the 79th Armoured Division and was replaced by Major General Brocas Burrows. The division was almost shipped to North Africa, but instead was re-equipped with M4 Sherman tanks.

Its armoured recce regiment went from armoured cars to light Centaur tanks and then to Cromwells. In December 1943 General Burrows was sent to Moscow and was replaced by Major General 'Pip' Roberts. It was under him that the 11th went to war. The division arrived in Normandy in June 1944. It fought in the battles of the Odon, Bourguebus Ridge, Mont Pincon, Neder Rijn and the Rhineland.

The division's insignia was a black bull with red eyes, horns and hooves on a yellow background.

11th Armoured Division 1941

Divisional Troops

27th Lancers: *Daimler and Humber armoured cars*

Royal Engineers:

12th Field Squadron, RE

13th Field Squadron, RE

147th Field Park Squadron, RE

29th Armoured Brigade:

23rd Hussars: *Valentines*

24th Lancers: *Valentines*

2nd Fife and Forfar Yeomanry: *Valentines*

8th Battalion, the Rifle Brigade

30th Armoured Brigade:

22nd Dragoons: *Valentines*

1st Lothian and Border Horse: *Valentines*

Westminister Dragoons: *Valentines*

2nd Battalion, Queen Westministers (March only)

12th Battalion, Kings Royal Rifle Corps (from March)

11th Support Group:

8th Battalion, Royal Ulster Rifles

12th Battalion, Green Howards

Royal Artillery:

13th Regiment Royal Horse Artillery

75th Anti-tank Regiment, RA

5th Light Anti-aircraft Regiment, RA

11th Armoured Division June 1942

Divisional Troops

27th Lancers: *Daimler and Humber armoured cars*

Royal Artillery:

13th Regiment Royal Horse Artillery

151st Field Regiment, RA: *24x25-pdr*

75th Anti-tank Regiment, RA

5th Light Anti-aircraft Regiment, RA

Royal Engineers:

12th Field Squadron, RE

13th Field Squadron, RE

147th Field Park Squadron, RE

29th Armoured Brigade:

23rd Hussars: *Crusaders*

24th Lancers: *Crusaders*

2nd Fife and Forfar Yeomanry: *Crusaders*

8th Battalion, the Rifle Brigade

159th Infantry Brigade:

4th Battalion, Kings Shropshire Light Infantry

1st Battalion, Hertfordshire Regiment

3rd Battalion, Monmouthshire Regiment

11th Armoured Division November 1943

Divisional Troops

2nd Northamptonshire Yeomanry: *Cromwells*

Royal Artillery:

13th Regiment Royal Horse Artillery: *24xSextons*

151st Field Regiment, RA: *24x25-pdr.*

75th Anti-tank Regiment, RA

5th Light Anti-aircraft Regiment, RA

Royal Engineers:

612th Field Squadron, RE

13th Field Squadron, RE

147th Field Park Squadron, RE

10th Bridging Troop, RE

29th Armoured Brigade:

23rd Hussars: *Shermans*

24th Lancers: *Shermans*

2nd Fife and Forfar Yeomanry: *Shermans*

8th Battalion, the Rifle Brigade

159th Infantry Brigade:

4th Battalion, Kings Shropshire Light Infantry

1st Battalion, Hertfordshire Regiment

3rd Battalion, Monmouthshire Regiment

11th Armoured Division August 1944

Divisional Troops

15th/19th Hussars: *Cromwells*

Royal Artillery:

13th Regiment Royal Horse Artillery: *24xSextons*

151st Field Regiment, RA: *25x25-pdr.*

75th Anti-tank Regiment, RA

5th Light Anti-aircraft Regiment, RA

Royal Engineers:

612th Field Squadron, RE

13th Field Squadron, RE

147th Field Park Squadron, RE

10th Bridging Troop, RE

29th Armoured Brigade:

23rd Hussars: *Sherman tanks*

3rd Royal Tank Regiment: *Sherman tanks*

2nd Fife and Forfar Yeomanry: *Sherman tanks*

8th Battalion, the Rifle Brigade

159th Infantry Brigade:

4th Battalion, Kings Shropshire Light Infantry

1st Battalion, Hertfordshire Regiment

3rd Battalion, Monmouthshire Regiment

42nd Armoured Division

The division formed from the 42nd East Lancashire Infantry Division in the United Kingdom. It disbanded in October 1943 never serving overseas.

The division's General Officer Commanding was at first Major-General Miles Dempsey and then afterwards it was Major-General Aldam Aizlewood.

The division's battle insignia was a white diamond with a thick red border.

42nd Armoured Division 1941

Divisional Troops

112nd Regiment RAC: *armoured cars*

Royal Engineers:

16th Field Squadron, RE

17th Field Squadron, RE

149th Field Park Squadron, RE

10th Armoured Brigade:

108th Regiment RAC: *Cruiser tanks*

109th Regiment RAC: *Cruiser tanks*

145th Regiment RAC: *Cruiser tanks*

13th Battalion, Highland Light Infantry

11th Armoured Brigade:

107th Regiment RAC: *Cruiser tanks*

110th Regiment RAC: *Cruiser tanks*

111th Regiment RAC: *Cruiser tanks*

1st Battalion, Highland Light Infantry

42nd Support Group:

1st Battalion, East Lancashire Regiment

Royal Artillery:

147th Field Regiment, RA

53rd Anti-tank Regiment, RA

93rd Light Anti-aircraft Regiment, RA

42nd Armoured Division March 1943

Divisional Troops

1st Northamptonshire Yeomanry

Royal Artillery:

86th Field Regiment, RA

147th Field Regiment, RA

53rd Anti-tank Regiment, RA

93rd Light Anti-aircraft Regiment, RA

Royal Engineers:

16th Field Squadron, RE

617th Field Squadron, RE

149th Field Park Squadron, RE

30th Armoured Brigade:

22nd Dragoons: *Sherman tanks*

1st Lothian and Border Horse: *Sherman tanks*

2nd County of London Yeomanry (Westminister Dragoons): *Sherman tanks*

12th Battalion, Kings Royal Rifle Corps

71st Infantry Brigade:

1st Battalion, East Lancashire Regiment

1st Battalion, Highland Light Infantry

1st Battalion, Oxfordshire and Buckinghamshire Light Infantry

79th Armoured Division

The division formed in August 1942 and reorganized in April 1943 as a specialized armour division that incorporated experimental tanks known as 'the Funnies'. These tanks were heavily involved in the D-Day invasion. Its tanks and specialized armour were used all through the Northwest Campaign and the division never fought as a traditional division.

The division never had any infantry or artillery, but it had five companies from the Royal Corps of Signals, two companies form the Royal Army Service Corps, two Ambulances from the Royal Army Medical Corps, four companies from the Royal Army Ordance Corps and ten light workshops from the Royal Electrical and Mechanical Engineers.

The division's only commander was Major General Sir P.C.S. Hobart.

The division's battle insignia was a black and white bulls head with red nostrils and horn tips all on an inverted black triangle in a yellow triangular frame.

79th Armoured Division 1942

Divisional Troops

162nd Regiment RAC: *armoured cars*

Royal Artillery:

142nd Field Regiment, RA

150th Field Regiment, RA

55th Anti-tank Regiment, RA

119th Light Anti-aircraft Regiment, RA

Royal Engineers:

18th Field Squadron, RE

19th Field Squadron, RE

508th Field Park Squadron, RE

27th Armoured Brigade:

4th/7th Dragoon Guards: *Crusaders*

13th/18th Hussars: *Covenanters and Crusaders*

1st East Riding Yeomanry: *Covenanters and M3 Stuarts*

185th Infantry Brigade:

2nd Battalion, Royal Warwickshire Regiment

2nd Battalion, Royal Norfolk Regiment

2nd Battalion, Kings Shropshire Light Infantry

79th Armoured Division January 1943

Divisional Troops

162nd Regiment RAC: *armoured cars*

Royal Artillery:

142nd Field Regiment, RA

150th Field Regiment, RA

55th Anti-tank Regiment, RA

119th Light Anti-aircraft Regiment, RA

Royal Engineers:

18th Field Squadron, RE

19th Field Squadron, RE

508th Field Park Squadron, RE

27th Armoured Brigade:

4th/7th Dragoon Guards

13th/18th Hussars

1st East Riding Yeomanry

185th Infantry Brigade:

2nd Battalion, Royal Warwickshire Regiment

2nd Battalion, Royal Norfolk Regiment

2nd Battalion, Kings Shropshire Light Infantry

79th Armoured Division June 1943

Divisional Troops

43rd Royal Tank Regiment: *WASPs and specialized armour*

Royal Engineers:

5th Assault Squadron, RE

6th Assault Squadron, RE

42nd Assault Squadron, RE

149th Field Park Squadron, RE

27th Armoured Brigade:

4th/7th Dragoon Guards

13th/18th Hussars

148th Regiment RAC

35th Tank Brigade:

49th Royal Tank Regiment

152nd Regiment RAC

155th Regiment RAC

79th Armoured Division November 1943

Divisional Troops

    43rd Royal Tank Regiment

1st Assault Brigade, RE

    5th Assault Regiment, RE

    6th Assault Regiment, RE

    42nd Assault Regiment, RE

    149th Assault Park Squadron, RE

35th Tank Brigade:

    49th Royal Tank Regiment

    152nd Regiment RAC

    155th Regiment RAC

Above: a modified Churchill tank known as the flame throwing Crocodile.

79th Armoured Division June 1944

1st Assault Brigade, RE

    5th Assault Regiment, RE: *AVRE (modified Churchills)*

    6th Assault Regiment, RE: *AVRE (modified Churchills)*

    42nd Assault Regiment, RE: *AVRE (modified Churchills)*

    149th Assault Park Squadron, RE: *AVRE (modified Churchills)*

    87th Assault Dozer Squadron, RE

30th Armoured Brigade:

    22nd Dragoons: *Sherman Flails (DD tanks)*

    1st Lothian and Border Horse: *Sherman Flails (DD tanks)*

    2nd County of London Yeomanry (Westminister Dragoons): *Sherman Flails (DD tanks)*

    141st Regiment RAC (The Buffs)

    11th Royal Tank Regiment

1st Tank Brigade:

    11th Royal Tank Regiment: *CDL*

    42nd Royal Tank Regiment: *CDL*

    45th Royal Tank Regiment: *CDL*

Divisional:

1st Canadian Armoured Carrier Regiment: *Kangaroos*

49th Armoured Carrier Regiment: *Kangaroos*

79th Armoured Division May 1945

1st Armoured Engineer Brigade, RE:

    5th Armoured Engineer Regiment, RE

    6th Armoured Engineer Regiment, RE

    42nd Armoured Engineer Regiment, RE

    149th Armoured Engineer Park Squadron, RE

    557th Armoured Engineer Training and Experiment Est.

30th Armoured Brigade:

    22nd Dragoons

    1st Lothian and Border Horse

    Westminister Dragoons

    141st Regiment RAC

    11th Royal Tank Regiment

1st Tank Brigade:

    11th Royal Tank Regiment

    42nd Royal Tank Regiment

    45th Royal Tank Regiment

31st Armoured Brigade:

    141st Regiment RAC (The Buffs)

    1st Fife and Forfar Yeomanry

    49th APC Regiment: *Kangaroos*

    1st Canadian APC Regiment: *Kangaroos*

    7th Royal Tank Regiment

    4th Royal Tank Regiment

33rd Armoured Brigade:

1st Northamptonshire Yeomanry

144th Regiment RAC

1st Bn East Riding Yeomanry

Staffordshire Yeomanry

Above: a Kangaroo at speed. They were basically tanks without the turret used for transporting infantry.

Guards Armoured Division

The division formed in the United Kingdom in 1941 with two brigades of Covenantor tanks. These were upgraded to 6-pdr. Crusaders and then one of the brigades was replaced by a lorried
infantry brigade. The remaining armoured brigades were
upgraded to M4 Sherman tanks and they were the tanks that the
division went to war with in 1944. The division landed in France
in June 1944. It fought all through the Normandy Campaign and
was the spearhead in Operation Garden in September 1944. It
fought until the end of the war and was reconstructed as an
infantry division in June 1945.

Unofficially the division formed four battle groups with each of
them matching an battalion of armour with an infantry battalion
from the same regiment with Royal Artillery and Royal
Engineers. It was the Irish Group that spearheaded Operation
Garden.

Major General Adair was the division's one and only General
Officer Commanding during the war.

The division's battle insignia was the ever seeing eye, a white
open eye on a blue shield with red trim.

Guards Armoured Division 1941

Divisional Troops

2nd Household Cavalry Regiment: *armoured cars*

Royal Engineers:

14th Field Squadron, RE

15th Field Squadron, RE

148th Field Park Squadron, RE

5th Guards Armoured Brigade:

2nd Bn. (Armoured) Grenadier Guards: *Convenantors*

1st Bn. (Armoured) Coldstream Guards: *Convenantors*

2nd Bn. (Armoured) Irish Guards: *Convenantors*

1st Bn. (Motor) Grenadier Guards

6th Guards Armoured Brigade:

4th Bn. (Armoured) Grenadier Guards: *Convenantors*

3rd Bn. (Armoured) Grenadier Guards: *Convenantors*

2nd Bn. (Armoured) Welsh Guards: *Convenantors*

4th Bn. (Motor) Coldstream Guards

Guards Support Group:

1st Bn. Welsh Guards

Royal Artillery:

153rd Field Regiment RA

21th Anti-tank Regiment, RA

94th Light Anti-aircraft Regiment, RA

Guards Armoured Division July 1942

Divisional Troops

    2nd Household Cavalry Regiment: *armoured cars*

    Royal Artillery:

        55th Field Regiment, RA

        153rd Field Regiment, RA

        21th Anti-tank Regiment, RA

        94th Light Anti-aircraft Regiment, RA

    Royal Engineers:

        14th Field Squadron, RE

        15th Field Squadron, RE

        148th Field Park Squadron, RE

5th Guards Armoured Brigade:

    2nd Bn. (Armoured) Grenadier Guards: *6pdr Crusaders*

    1st Bn. (Armoured) Coldstream Guards: *6pdr Crusaders*

    2nd Bn. (Armoured) Irish Guards: *6pdr Crusaders*

    1st Bn. (Motor) Grenadier Guards

32nd Guards Infantry Brigade:

    5th Bn. Coldstream Guards

    4th Bn. Scots Guards

    1st Bn. Welsh Guards

Guards Armoured Division April 1943

Divisional Troops

2nd Bn. (Armoured) Welsh Guards

Royal Artillery:

55th Field Regiment, RA

153rd Field Regiment, RA

21th Anti-tank Regiment, RA

94th Light Anti-aircraft Regiment, RA

Royal Engineers:

14th Field Squadron, RE

615th Field Squadron, RE

148th Field Park Squadron, RE

5th Guards Armoured Brigade:

2nd Bn. (Armoured Grenadier Guards: *Sherman tanks*

1st Bn. (Armoured) Coldstream Guards: *Sherman tanks*

2nd Bn. (Armoured) Irish Guards: *Sherman tanks*

1st Bn. (Motor) Grenadier Guards

32nd Guards Infantry Brigade:

5th Bn. Coldstream Guards

4th Bn. Scots Guards

1st Bn. Welsh Guards

Guards Armoured Division 1944

Divisional Troops

    2nd Bn. (Armoured) Welsh Guards: *Cromwells and Challengers*

    Royal Artillery:

        55th Field Regiment, RA

        153rd Field Regiment, RA

        21th Anti-tank Regiment, RA

        94th Light Anti-aircraft Regiment, RA

    Royal Engineers:

        14th Field Squadron, RE

        615th Field Squadron, RE

        148th Field Park Squadron, RE

        11th Bridging Troop, RE

5th Guards Armoured Brigade:

    2nd Bn. (Armoured) Grenadier Guards: *Sherman tanks*

    1st Bn. (Armoured) Coldstream Guards: *Sherman tanks*

    2nd Bn. (Armoured) Irish Guards: *Sherman tanks*

    1st Bn. (Motor) Grenadier Guards

32nd Guards Infantry Brigade:

    5th Bn. Coldstream Guards

    3rd Bn. Irish Guards

    1st Bn. Welsh Guards

Guards Armoured Division 1945

Divisional Troops

2nd Bn. (Armoured) Welsh Guards: *Cromwells and Challengers*

Royal Artillery:

55th Field Regiment, RA

153rd Field Regiment, RA

21th Anti-tank Regiment, RA

94th Light Anti-aircraft Regiment, RA

Royal Engineers:

14th Field Squadron, RE

615th Field Squadron, RE

148th Field Park Squadron, RE

11th Bridging Troop, RE

5th Guards Armoured Brigade:

2nd Bn. (Armoured) Grenadier Guards: *Sherman tanks*

1st Bn. (Armoured) Coldstream Guards: *Sherman tanks*

2nd Bn. (Armoured) Irish Guards: *Sherman tanks*

1st Bn. (Motor) Grenadier Guards

32nd Guards Infantry Brigade:

5th Bn. Coldstream Guards

2nd Bn. Scots Guards

1st Bn. Welsh Guards

Above: a Sherman tank of the Royal Scot Greys on April 4th, 1945 at the Dort-mund-Ems Canal.

The Mixed Divisions

The mixed divisions were regular infantry divisions with one of its three infantry brigades replaced by a tank brigade consisting of infantry tanks. The reasoning for this was to improve tank-infantry coordination. Between May 1942 and January 1943 the following seven infantry divisions were converted to mixed:

1st

3rd

4th

15th (Scottish)

43rd (Wessex)

53rd (Welsh)

77th

Only the 4th Mixed Division saw action as a mixed division. All seven Mixed Divisions were converted back to infantry divisions by December 1943 at the latest.

The Supporting Arms and Services were the same as the Armoured Divisions.

Typical Mixed Division

<u>Divisional Troops:</u>

Armoured Recce Regiment

MG or Support Battalion

Royal Artillery:

Field Artillery Regiment, RA

Field Artillery Regiment, RA

Field Artillery Regiment, RA

Anti-tank Regiment, RA

Light Anti-aircraft Regiment, RA

Royal Engineers:

Field Company, RE

Field Company, RE

Field Company, RE

Field Park Company, RE

<u>Infantry Brigade:</u>

Infantry Battalion

Infantry Battalion

Infantry Battalion

<u>Infantry Brigade:</u>

Infantry Battalion

Infantry Battalion

Infantry Battalion

<u>Tank Brigade:</u>

Tank Battalion

Tank Battalion

Tank Battalion

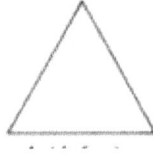

1st Mixed Division

The regular division in September 1939, served in Belgium and France in 1940 and converted to a mixed division on June 1942 by replacing one of its brigades with the 34th Tank Brigade. Three months later the tank brigade was replaced by the 25th Tank Brigade in November and the division converted back to an infantry division in December 1942. None of the Royal Artillery or Royal Engineers units seemed to have been affected by either change.

The division's battle insignia was the white triangle and its General Officer Commanding through this period was Major General Walter Clutterbuck.

1st Mixed Division June 1942

Divisional Troops:

    1st Regiment Recce Corps

    4th Battalion, Cheshire Regiment (MG)

    Royal Artillery:

        2nd Field Artillery Regiment, RA

        19th Field Artillery Regiment, RA

        67th Field Artillery Regiment, RA

        81st Anti-tank Regiment, RA

        90th Light Anti-aircraft Regiment, RA

    Royal Engineers:

        23rd Field Company, RE

        238th Field Company, RE

        248th Field Company, RE

        6th Field Park Company, RE

2nd Infantry Brigade:

    1st Battalion, Loyal Regiment

    2nd Battalion, North Staffordshire Regiment

    1st Battalion, Gordon Highlanders

3rd Infantry Brigade:

    1st Battalion, Duke of Wellington Regiment

    2nd Battalion, Foresters

    1st Battalion, King's Shropshire Light Infantry

34th Tank Brigade:

    North Irish Horse: *Churchill tanks*

    147th Regiment RAC: *Churchill tanks*

    153rd Regiment RAC: *Churchill tanks*

1st Mixed Division September 1942

Divisional Troops:

    1st Regiment Recce Corps

    4th Battalion, Cheshire Regiment (MG)

    Royal Artillery:

        2nd Field Artillery Regiment, RA

        19th Field Artillery Regiment, RA

        67th Field Artillery Regiment, RA

        81st Anti-tank Regiment, RA

        90th Light Anti-aircraft Regiment, RA

    Royal Engineers:

        23rd Field Company, RE

        238th Field Company, RE

        248th Field Company, RE

        6th Field Park Company, RE

2nd Infantry Brigade:

    1st Battalion, Loyal Regiment

    2nd Battalion, North Staffordshire Regiment

    1st Battalion, Gordon Highlanders

3rd Infantry Brigade:

    1st Battalion, Duke of Wellington Regiment

    2nd Battalion, Foresters

    1st Battalion, King's Shropshire Light Infantry

25th Tank Brigade:

    North Irish Horse: *Churchill tanks*

    51st Royal Tank Regiment: *Churchill tanks*

    153rd Regiment RAC: *Churchill tanks*

Above: a Churchill infantry tank during a practice beach landing .

3rd Mixed Division

The division was a regular division in September 1939, fought in France and Belgium in 1940 and then converted to a mixed division by substituting one of its infantry brigades with the 33rd Tank Brigade. The brigade stayed with the division until April 1943 when the division converted back to an infantry division. The only effect that it had on the rest of the division was that its Machine Gun Battalion was renamed a Support Battalion during this time. It was renamed a Machine Gun Battalion afterwards.

 The 3rd Infantry Division landed on D-Day and fought in Northwest Europe in 1944 and 1945.

The division's insignia was a red inverted triangle within a black triangle. The General Commanding Officers during this period were Major General Eric Hayes and then Major General Ramsden.

3rd Mixed Division July 1942

Divisional Troops:

3rd Regiment Recce Corps

2nd Battalion, Middlesex Regiment (MG)

Royal Artillery:

>7th Field Artillery Regiment, RA
>
>76th Field Artillery Regiment, RA
>
>33rd Field Artillery Regiment, RA
>
>20th Anti-tank Regiment, RA
>
>92nd Light Anti-aircraft Regiment, RA

Royal Engineers:

>246th Field Company, RE
>
>17th Field Company, RE
>
>253rd Field Company, RE
>
>15th Field Park Company, RE

33rd Tank Brigade:

43rd Royal Tank Regiment: *Churchill tanks*

144th Regiment RAC: *Churchill tanks*

148th Regiment RAC: *Churchill tanks*

8th Infantry Brigade:

1st Battalion, Suffolk Regiment

2nd Battalion, East Yorkshire Regiment

2nd Battalion, Gloucestershire Regiment

9th Infantry Brigade:

2nd Battalion, Lincolnshire Regiment

1st Battalion, Kings Own Scottish Borderers

2nd Battalion, Royal Ulster Rifles

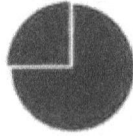

4th Mixed Division

A regular division in September 1939, fought in France in Belgium in 1940, became a mixed division in June 1942, where it fought in the Tunisian Campaign under Major General John Hawkesworth and then converted back to an infantry in December 1943. As an infantry division it fought in Italy and ended the war in Greece.

The division's insignia was a red circle with a quadrant protruding on a white background.

4th Mixed Division June 1942

Divisional Troops:

4th Regiment Recce Corps

2nd Royal Northumberland Fusiliers (MG)

Royal Artillery:

77th Field Artillery Regiment, RA

22nd Field Artillery Regiment, RA

30th Field Artillery Regiment, RA

14th Anti-tank Regiment, RA

91st Light Anti-aircraft Regiment, RA

Royal Engineers:

7th Field Company, RE

225th Field Company, RE

59th Field Company, RE

18th Field Park Company, RE

10th Infantry Brigade:

2nd Battalion, Bedfordshire and Hertfordshire Regiment

2nd Battalion, Duke of Cornwalls Light Infantry

1/6th Battalion, East Surrey Regiment

21st Tank Brigade:

12th Royal Tank Regiment: *Churchill tanks*

48th Royal Tank Regiment: *Churchill tanks*

145th Royal Tank Regiment: *Churchill tanks*

12th Infantry Brigade:

2nd Battalion, Royal Fusiliers

1st Battalion, South Lancashire Regiment

1st Battalion, Black Watch

15th (Scottish) Mixed Division

The division was a second line Territorial division in September 1939, being a duplicate of the 52nd (Lowland) Infantry Division. It officially started on September 2nd, 1939 where all of its units were scattered over Scotland and were short of weapons and equipment. In April 1940 the division was put into the defenses in Southern England where a German invasion could be expected daily. It still had lower scale of small arms, which meant only 8 LMGs per battalion and old artillery pieces for the RA regiments. Throughout 1941 the division trained hard and received the proper equipment and was becoming a division of high standard. Unfortunately, it was placed on a lower establishment in November 1941 and the division was drained for reinforcements for other units. Several battalions left the division; the 7th KOSB converted to glider troops and the 11th HLI converted to tanks.

Morale sunk until the division was back onto the Higher Established and was reorganized as a mixed division in March 1943 where the 15th Infantry Brigade was replaced by the 6th Guards Armoured Brigade. Two months later they were replaced by the 6th Guards Tank Brigade who only stayed until September 1943, ending the 15th Mixed Division's days. The 227th Infantry Brigade joined and the division trained and was fully ashore in Normandy by June 24th, 1944. The division served throughout Northwest Europe and ended the war in Germany.

The division's General Officer during its days as a mixed division was Major General D.C. Bullen-Smith. Its insignia was a silver thistle within a silver disk on a dark blue background.

15th (Scottish) Mixed Division January 1943

Divisional Troops:

15th Indp. Coy/Sqn. Recce Corps

Royal Artillery:

181st Field Artillery Regiment, RA

190th Field Artillery Regiment, RA

131st Field Artillery Regiment, RA

97th Anti-tank Regiment, RA

119th Light Anti-aircraft Regiment, RA

Royal Engineers:

278th Field Company, RE

279th Field Company, RE

624th Field Park Company, RE

44th Infantry Brigade:

8th Battalion, Royal Scots

6th Battalion, Kings Own Scottish Borderers

7th Battalion, Kings Own Scottish Borderers

6th Guards Armoured Brigade:

3rd (Armoured) Battalion, Grenadier Guards: *Churchill tanks*

4th (Armoured) Battalion, Grenadier Guards: *Churchill tanks*

2nd (Armoured) Battalion, Welsh Guards: *Churchill tanks*

46th Infantry Brigade:

2nd Battalion, Glasgow Highlanders

7th Battalion, Seaforth Highlanders

9th Battalion, Cameroonians

15th (Scottish) Mixed Division March 1943

Divisional Troops:

    15th Regiment Recce Corps

    Royal Artillery:

        181st Field Artillery Regiment, RA

        190th Field Artillery Regiment, RA

        131st Field Artillery Regiment, RA

        97th Anti-tank Regiment, RA

        119th Light Anti-aircraft Regiment, RA

    Royal Engineers:

        20th Field Company, RE (from April)

        278th Field Company, RE

        279th Field Company, RE

        624th Field Park Company, RE

44th Infantry Brigade:

    8th Battalion, Royal Scots

    6th Battalion, Kings Own Scottish Borderers

    7th Battalion, Kings Own Scottish Borderers

6th Guards Tank Brigade:

    4th Tank Battalion, Grenadier Guards: *Churchill tanks*

    4th Tank Battalion, Coldstream Guards: *Churchill tanks*

    10th Tank Battalion, Scots Guards: *Churchill tanks*

46th Infantry Brigade:

    2nd Battalion, Glasgow Highlanders

    7th Battalion, Seaforth Highlanders

    9th Battalion, Cameroonians

43rd (Wessex) Mixed Division

The division was a first line Territorial Infantry Division in September 1939. It organized as a mixed division from June 1942 to September 1943. In September 1942 it swapped its tank brigade with the 1st Mixed Division's tank brigade.

The General Officer Commanding during this period was Major General Gwilym Ivor Thomas. Its insignia was gold wyvern on a blue background.

43rd (Wessex) Mixed Division June 1942

Divisional Troops:

    43rd Regiment Recce Corps

    1/8th Battalion, Middlesex Regiment (MG)

    Royal Artillery:

        94th Field Artillery Regiment, RA

        112th Field Artillery Regiment, RA

        179th Field Artillery Regiment, RA

        59th Anti-tank Regiment, RA

        110th Light Anti-aircraft Regiment, RA

    Royal Engineers:

        204th Field Company, RE

        260th Field Company, RE

        553rd Field Company, RE

        207th Field Park Company, RE

129th Infantry Brigade:

    4th Battalion, Somerset Light Infantry

    4th Battalion, Wiltshire Regiment

    5th Battalion, Wiltshire Regiment

130th Infantry Brigade:

    7th Battalion, Hampshire Regiment

    4th Battalion, Dorset Regiment

    5th Battalion, Dorset Regiment

25th Tank Brigade:

    51st Royal Tank Regiment: *Churchill tanks*

    11th Royal Tank Regiment: *Churchill tanks*

    142nd Regiment RAC: *Churchill tanks*

43rd (Wessex) Mixed Division September 1942

Divisional Troops:

43rd Regiment Recce Corps

1/8th Battalion, Middlesex Regiment (MG)

Royal Artillery:

94th Field Artillery Regiment, RA

112th Field Artillery Regiment, RA

179th Field Artillery Regiment, RA

59th Anti-tank Regiment, RA

110th Light Anti-aircraft Regiment, RA

Royal Engineers:

204th Field Company, RE

260th Field Company, RE

553rd Field Company, RE

207th Field Park Company, RE

129th Infantry Brigade:

4th Battalion, Somerset Light Infantry

4th Battalion, Wiltshire Regiment

5th Battalion, Wiltshire Regiment

130th Infantry Brigade:

7th Battalion, Hampshire Regiment

4th Battalion, Dorset Regiment

5th Battalion, Dorset Regiment

34th Tank Brigade:

147th Regiment RAC: *Churchill tanks*

151st Regiment RAC: *Churchill tanks*

153rd Regiment RAC: *Churchill tanks*

53rd (Welsh) Mixed Division

The division was a first line Territorial Infantry Division in September 1939. It organized as a mixed division from May 1942 to October 1943. It fought in Normandy, the Netherlands and Germany.

The General Officer Commanding during this period was Major General Gerald C. Bucknall. Its insignia was a red 'W' on a green background.

53rd (Wessex) Mixed Division June 1942

Divisional Troops:

53rd Battalion Recce Corps

5th Battalion, Cheshire Regiment (MG)

Royal Artillery:

81st Field Artillery Regiment, RA

83rd Field Artillery Regiment, RA

133rd Field Artillery Regiment, RA

71st Anti-tank Regiment, RA

116th Light Anti-aircraft Regiment, RA

Royal Engineers:

244th Field Company, RE

282nd Field Company, RE

555th Field Company, RE

285th Field Park Company, RE

158th Infantry Brigade:

4th Battalion, Royal Welch Fusiliers

6th Battalion, Royal Welch Fusiliers

7th Battalion, Royal Welch Fusiliers

160th Infantry Brigade:

4th Battalion, Welch Regiment

1/5th Battalion, Welch Regiment

2nd Battalion, Mommouthshire Regiment

31st Tank Brigade:

9th Royal Tank Regiment: *Churchill tanks*

10th Royal Tank Regiment: *Churchill tanks* (left Feb. 1943)

141st Regiment RAC: *Churchill tanks*

7th Royal Tank Regiment: *Churchill tanks* (from Feb. 1943)

77th Mixed Division

The division formed from the Devon and Cornwall County Division and was put onto the Lower Establishment in December 1941. It was redesignated 77th Infantry (Reserve) Division in December 1942 and then was converted to a mixed division in January 1943 by exchanging its 211st Infantry Brigade for the 11th Tank Brigade. The Division disbanded in September 1944.

The General Officer Commanding during this period was Major General Godwin Michelmare. Its insignia was a red sword held aloft by a white arm emerging from three blue wavy lines on a black background.

77th Mixed Division January 1943

Divisional Troops:

77th Squadron Recce Corps

10th Battalion, Kings Royal Rifle Corps (Motor)

Royal Artillery:

176th Field Artillery Regiment, RA

Royal Engineers:

566th Field Company, RE

203rd Infantry Brigade:

10th Battalion, Royal Sussex

1/5th Battalion, Queens Royal Regiment

8th Battalion, Devonshire Regiment

209th Infantry Brigade:

9th Battalion, Buffs (Royal East Kent Regiment)

10th Battalion, Buffs (Royal East Kent Regiment)

11th Battalion, Hampshire Regiment

11th Tank Brigade:

107th Regiment RAC: *Churchill tanks*

110th Regiment RAC: *Churchill tanks*

111th Regiment RAC: *Churchill tanks*

Abbreviations:

AB   Armoured Brigade

AD   Armoured Division

AVRE   Armoured Vehicle Royal Engineers

BEF   British Expeditionary Force

Bn.   Battalion

CDL   Canal Defense Light

Div   Division

Est.   Establishment

Gds   Guards

Gp   Group

Lt.   Light

LMG   Light Machine Gun

MD   Mixed Division

Pdr   Pounder

RA   Royal Artillery

RAC   Royal Armoured Corps

RE   Royal Engineers

RHA   Royal Horse Artillery

Sqn.   Squadron

Sources:

The Black Bull: From Normandy to the Baltic with the 11th Armoured Division by Patrick Delaforce

British Guards Armoured Division 1941-43 by John Sanders

British Battle Insignia 2 1939-45 by Mike Chappell

British Light Tanks 1927-45 Mark I-VI by David Fletcher and Henry Morshead

Crusader and Covenanter Cruiser Tanks 1939-45 by David Fletcher and Peter Sarson

Desert Rats: British 8th Army in North Africa 1941-43 by Tim Moreman

Divisions of the British Army 1939-1945 2nd Edition by Malcolm A. Bellis

From D-Day to VE-Day The British Soldier Vol. 2 Organization, Tanks and Vehicles by Jean Bouchery

The Guards Divisions 1914-45 by Mike Chappell

The History of the 4th Armoured Brigade by Brig. R.M.P. Carver July 1945

The Illustrated Encyclopedia of 20th Century Weapons and Warfare Volumes 1 to 24 (1967)

Irish Regiments in the World Wars by David Murphy and Gerry Embleton

Regimental Museum of The Buffs (Royal East Kent Regiment)

Scottish Units in the World Wars by Mike Chappell

Tnak Force: Allied Amour in World War II by Kenneth Mackey

Valentine Infantry Tank 1938-45 by Bruce Oliver Newsome and H. Morshead

Index/List of Units

27th Armoured Brigade	- 9AD, 79AD	61, 81-83
28th Armoured Brigade	- 9AD	61-63
29th Armoured Brigade	- 11AD	73-76
30th Armoured Brigade	- 11AD,42AD,79AD	73,79,85,86
31st Armoured Brigade	- 79AD	86
31st Tank Brigade	- 53MD	113
32nd (Guards) Infantry Brigade	- Gds	90-93
33rd Armoured Brigade	- 79AD	87
33rd Tank Brigade	- 3MD	103
34th Tank Brigade	- 1MD, 43MD	99, 111
35th Tank Brigade	- 79AD	83, 84
38th (Irish) Infantry Brigade	- 6AD	45
44th Infantry Brigade	- 15MD	107, 108
46th Infantry Brigade	- 15MD	107, 108
61st Infantry Brigade	- 6AD	47
71st Infantry Brigade	- 42AD	79
129th Infantry Brigade	- 43MD	110, 111
130th Infantry Brigade	- 43MD	110, 111
131st Infantry Brigade	- 7AD	54, 55
133rd Lorried Infantry Brigade	- 10AD	68
158th Infantry Brigade	- 53MD	113
159th Infantry Brigade	- 11AD	74-76
160th Infantry Brigade	- 53MD	113
161st Indian Motor Brigade Group	- 10AD	66
185th Infantry Brigade	- 79AD	81, 82
200th Guards Brigade	- 1AD	34
201st Guards Brigade	- 1AD, 10AD	69
203rd Infantry Brigade	- 77MD	115
209th Infantry Brigade	- 77MD	115
1st Armoured Engineer Brigade, RE	- 79AD	86
Light Armoured Brigade (Egypt)	- 7AD	49
Heavy Armoured Brigade (Egypt)	- 7AD	49

Armour Battalions:

1st (Armoured) Battalion, Coldstream Guards	89-93
4th Tank Battalion, Coldstream Guards	108
2nd (Armoured) Battalion, Grenadier Guards	89-93
3rd (Armoured) Battalion, Grenadier Guards	89, 107
2nd (Armoured) Battalion, Irish Guards	89-93
4th (Armoured/Tank) Battalion, Grenadier Guards	89, 107, 108
10th Tank Battalion, Scots Guards	108
4th/7th Dragoon Guards	61, 80-83
1st Royal Dragoons	68
5th Royal Inniskilling Dragoon Guards	55, 61-63
Kings Dragoon Guards	39-41
2nd (Armoured) Battalion, Welsh Guards	89, 91-93, 107
22nd Dragoons	73, 79, 85-86
Westminister Dragoons (2nd County of London Yeomanry)	73, 79, 85, 86
3rd King's Own Hussars	39-41, 68, 69
4th Hussars	37, 39-41
7th Hussars	49-51, 70
8th Kings Royal Irish Hussars	49-52, 55
10th Hussars Armoured Regiment	31-37
11th Hussars	49-54
13th/18th Hussars	61, 80-83
23rd Hussars	73-76
Yorkshire Hussars	65-67
15th/19th Hussars	61-63, 76
1st Royal Gloucestershire Hussars	43, 44, 49, 63
2nd Royal Gloucestershire Hussars	33, 39, 40, 53
North Irish Horse	99, 100
1st Lothian and Border Horse	73, 79, 85, 86
2nd Lothian and Border Horse	43-47
1st Household Cavalry Regiment	65-67, 69
2nd Household Cavalry Regiment	89-90
9th Lancers Armoured Regiment	31-37
24th Lancers	73, 75
16th/5th Lancers	43-47
12th Lancers	32-37
17th/21st Lancers	43-47
27th Lancers	73, 74
107th Regiment RAC	78, 115

108th Regiment RAC	78
109th Regiment RAC	78
110th Regiment RAC	78, 115
111th Regiment RAC	78, 115
112th Regiment RAC	78
141st Regiment RAC (The Buffs)	85, 86, 113
142nd Regiment RAC	110
144th Regiment RAC	87, 103
145th Regiment RAC	78
147th Regiment RAC	99, 111
148th Regiment RAC	83, 103
151st Regiment RAC	111
152nd Regiment RAC	83, 84
153rd Regiment RAC	99, 100, 111
155th Regiment RAC	83, 84
162nd Regiment RAC	81, 82
1st Royal Tank Regiment	49-51, 54, 55
2nd Royal Tank Regiment	31, 32, 50, 51, 70
3rd Royal Tank Regiment	31, 32, 41, 52, 67, 68, 76
4th Royal Tank Regiment	51, 86
5th Royal Tank Regiment	31, 32, 41, 52, 54, 55
6th Royal Tank Regiment	41, 49-51, 70
7th Royal Tank Regiment	86, 113
8th Royal Tank Regiment	51, 70
9th Royal Tank Regiment	113
10th Royal Tank Regiment	113
11th Royal Tank Regiment	85-87, 110
12th Royal Tank Regiment	105
40th Royal Tank Regiment	57, 58, 71
41st Royal Tank Regiment	57-59
42nd Royal Tank Regiment	51, 85, 86
43rd Royal Tank Regiment	83, 84, 103
44th Royal Tank Regiment	51
45th Royal Tank Regiment	57-59, 85, 86
46th Royal Tank Regiment	57, 58, 71
47th Royal Tank Regiment	57-59
48th Royal Tank Regiment	105
49th Royal Tank Regiment	83, 84
50th Royal Tank Regiment	57, 58, 71
51st Royal Tank Regiment	100, 110
145th Royal Tank Regiment	105
152nd Royal Tank Regiment	84
155th Royal Tank Regiment	84
1st Derbyshire Yeomanry	43-47
2nd Derbyshire Yeomanry	57 59

1st East Riding Yeomanry	61,80-82, 87
1st Fife and Forfar Yeomanry	61-63, 86
1st Northamptonshire Yeomanry	43, 44, 79, 87
2nd Fife and Forfar Yeomanry	73-76
2nd Northamptonshire Yeomanry	43, 44, 75
3rd County of London Yeomanry	33, 39, 40, 53
4th Country of London Yeomanry	33, 39, 40, 53, 54
Royal Wiltshire Yeomanry	65-69
Staffordshire Yeomanry	65-68, 87
Warwickshire Yeomanry	65-68
Notts (Sherwood Rangers) Yeomanry	65-68
Inns of the Court Regiment	61, 62
Queen's Bays Armoured Regiment	31-37
Royal Scots Greys	65, 66, 94
49th APC Regiment	85, 86
1st Canadian APC Regiment	85, 86
1st Regiment Recce Corps	99, 100
3rd Regiment Recce Corps	103
4th Regiment Recce Corps	103
15th Indp. Coy./Sqn. Recce Corps	107
43rd Regiment Recce Corps	110, 111
53rd Regiment Recce Corps	113
77th Squadron Recce Corps	115

Infantry Battalions:

1st Argyll and Sutherland Highlanders   66

2nd Battalion, Bedfordshire and Hertfordshire Regiment   106
1st Battalion, Black Watch   106
4th Battalion, Borders   32, 33
1st Battalion, Buffs (Royal East Kent Regiment)   35-37, 53, 67, 68
4th Battalion, Buffs (Royal East Kent Regiment)   68
9th Battalion, Buffs (Royal East Kent Regiment)   115
10th Battalion, Buffs (Royal East Kent Regiment)   115

9th Battalion, Cameroonians   107, 108
4th Battalion, Cheshire Regiment (MG)   99, 100
5th Battalion ,Cheshire Regiment (MG)   113
2nd Battalion, Coldstream Guards   34, 46, 69
3rd Battalion, Coldstream Guards   34, 69
4th Battalion, Coldstream Guards   89
5th Battalion, Coldstream Guards   90-93

4th Battalion, Dorset Regiment   110, 111
5th Battalion, Dorset Regiment   110, 111
2nd Battalion, Devonshire Regiment   55
8th Battalion, Devonshire Regiment   115
1st Battalion, Duke of Cornwalls Light Infantry   66
2nd Battalion, Duke of Cornwalls Light Infantry   106
1st Battalion, Duke of Wellington Regiment   99, 100
9th Battalion, Durham Light Infantry   55

1st Battalion, East Lancashire Regiment   78, 79
1/6th Battalion, East Surrey Regiment   106
2/6th Battalion, East Surrey Regiment   62, 63
2nd Battalion, East Yorkshire Regiment   103

2nd Battalion, Foresters   99, 100
9th Battalion, Foresters   34
14th Battalion, Foresters   35-37, 53, 57, 58

2nd Battalion, Glasgow Highlanders   107, 108
2nd Battalion, Gloucestershire Regiment   103
1st Battalion, Gordon Highlanders   99, 100
1st (Motor) Battalion, Grenadier Guards   89-93
3rd Battalion, Grenadier Guards   46
6th Battalion, Grenadier Guards   69
12th Battalion, Green Howards   73

7th Battalion, Hampshire Regiment	110, 111
11th Battalion, Hampshire Regiment	115
1st Battalion, Herfordshire Regiment	74-76
1st Battalion, Highland Light Infantry	78, 79
13th Battalion, Highland Light Infantry	78
1st Battalion, Kings Own Scottish Borderers	103
6th Battalion, Kings Own Scottish Borderers	107, 108
7th Battalion, Kings Own Scottish Borderers	107, 108
9th Battalion, Kings Own Yorkshire Light Infantry	35-37, 53
1st Battalion, Kings Royal Rifle Corps	32-37, 50-52, 71
2nd Battalion, Kings Royal Rifle Corps	31, 33, 34, 70
8th Battalion, Kings Royal Rifle Corps	61-63
9th Battalion, Kings Royal Rifle Corps	52
10th Battalion, Kings Royal Rifle Corps (Motor)	44, 115
11th Battalion, Kings Royal Rifle Corps	59, 68, 69
12th Battalion, Kings Royal Rifle Corps	73, 79
1st Battalion, King's Shropshire Light Infantry	99, 100
2nd Battalion, Kings Shropshire Light Infantry	81, 82
4th Battalion, Kings Shropshire Light Infantry	74-76
2nd Battalion, Lincolnshire Regiment	103
2nd Battalion, London Irish Rifles	45
1st Battalion, Loyal Regiment	99, 100
1/8th Battalion, Middlesex Regiment (MG)	110, 111
2nd Battalion, Monmouthshire Regiment	113
3rd Battalion, Monmouthshire Regiment (MG)	74-76
2nd Battalion, North Staffordshire Regiment	99, 100
1st Bn. Oxfordshire and Buckinghamshire Light Infantry 79	
9th Battalion, Queen's Own Rifles (West Kent Regiment) 44	
1/5th Battalion, Queen's Royal Regiment	54, 55, 115
1/6th Battalion, Queen's Royal Regiment	54
1/7th Battalion, Queen's Royal Regiment	54
1st Battalion, Queen Victoria Rifles	61
2nd Battalion, Queen Victoria Rifles	61
1st Battalion, Queen Westminsters	57, 58
2nd Battalion, Queen Westminsters	73
1st Battalion, Rangers Regiment	39-41
2nd Battalion, Rangers Regiment	43
2nd Battalion, Royal Fusiliers	106
1st Battalion, Royal Irish Rifles	45
1st Battalion, the Rifle Brigade	31, 54, 55

Royal Artillery:

1st Regiment Royal Horse Artillery	31, 67-70
2nd Regiment Royal Horse Artillery	31, 34-37, 39-41
3rd Regiment Royal Horse Artillery	50-55
4th Regiment Royal Horse Artillery	35, 36, 50-55
5th Regiment Royal Horse Artillery	57-59
6th Regiment Royal Horse Artillery	61-63
11th Regiment Royal Horse Artillery	32-37
12th Regiment Royal Horse Artillery	39-40, 43-47
13th Regiment Royal Horse Artillery	73-76
104th Regiment Royal Horse Artillery	41, 68-70
2nd Field Artillery Regiment, RA	99, 100
7th Field Artillery Regiment, RA	103
19th Field Artillery Regiment, RA	99, 100
22nd Field Artillery Regiment, RA	105
30th Field Artillery Regiment, RA	105
33rd Field Artillery Regiment, RA	103
55th Field Artillery Regiment, RA	90-93
67th Field Artillery Regiment, RA	99, 100
76th Field Artillery Regiment, RA	103
77th Field Artillery Regiment, RA	105
81st Field Artillery Regiment, RA	113
83rd Field Artillery Regiment, RA	113
86th Field Artillery Regiment, RA	79
94th Field Artillery Regiment, RA	110, 111
98th Field Artillery Regiment, RA	68
112th Field Artillery Regiment, RA	110, 111
131th Field Artillery Regiment, RA	107, 108
133rd Field Artillery Regiment, RA	113
141st Field Regiment, RA	62, 63
142nd Field Regiment, RA	81, 82
146th Field Regiment, RA	59
147th Field Regiment, RA	78, 79
150th Field Regiment, RA	81, 82
151st Field Regiment, RA	74-76
152nd Field Regiment, RA	45-47
153rd Field Regiment, RA	89-93
176th Field Regiment, RA	115
179th Field Artillery Regiment, RA	110, 111
181st Field Artillery Regiment, RA	107, 108
190th Field Artillery Regiment, RA	107, 108
14th Anti-tank Regiment, RA	105
20th Anti-tank Regiment, RA	103

21st Anti-tank Regiment, RA	89-93
53rd Anti-tank Regiment, RA	78, 79
55th Anti-tank Regiment, RA	81, 82
59th Anti-tank Regiment, RA	110, 111
60th Anti-tank Regiment, RA	31, 50-55
71st Anti-tank Regiment, RA	113
72nd Anti-tank Regiment, RA	43-47
73rd Anti-tank Regiment, RA	57-59
74th Anti-tank Regiment, RA	61-63
75th Anti-tank Regiment, RA	73-76
76th Anti-tank Regiment, RA	33-37
81st Anti-tank Regiment, RA	99, 100
84th Anti-tank Regiment, RA	68-70
97th Anti-tank Regiment, RA	107, 108
1st Light Anti-aircraft Regiment, RA	51-55
5th Light Anti-aircraft Regiment, RA	73-76
15th Light Anti-aircraft Regiment, RA	41
Battery/38th Light Anti-aircraft Regiment	51
42nd Light Anti-aircraft Regiment, RA	35-37
51st Light Anti-aircraft Regiment, RA	44-47
53rd Light Anti-aircraft Regiment, RA	68, 69
54th Light Anti-aircraft Regiment, RA	61-63
56th Light Anti-aircraft Regiment, RA	58, 59
61st Light Anti-aircraft Regiment, RA	33
90th Light Anti-aircraft Regiment, RA	99, 100
91st Light Anti-aircraft Regiment, RA	105
92nd Light Anti-aircraft Regiment, RA	103
93rd Light Anti-aircraft Regiment, RA	78, 79
94th Light Anti-aircraft Regiment, RA	89-93
101st Light Anti-aircraft/Anti-tank Regiment, RA	32
101st Light Anti-aircraft Regiment, RA	70
102nd Light Anti-aircraft/Anti-tank Regiment, RA	39-41
110th Light Anti-aircraft Regiment, RA	110, 111
116th Light Anti-aircraft Regiment, RA	113
119th Light Anti-aircraft Regiment, RA	81-82, 107, 108
44th Light Anti-aircraft Battery	34
88th Light Anti-aircraft Battery	34
116th Light AA Battery, RA	59

Royal Engineers:

5th Armoured Engineer Regiment, RE	86
6th Armoured Engineer Regiment, RE	86
42nd Armoured Engineer Regiment, RE	86
149th Armoured Engineer Park Squadron, RE	86
557th Armoured Engineer Training and Experiment Est.	86
5th Assault Regiment, RE	83-85
6th Assault Regiment, RE	83-85
42nd Assault Regiment, RE	83-85
149th Assault Park Squadron, RE	83-85
87th Assault Dozer Squadron, RE	85
1st Field Squadron, RE	32-37
2nd Field Squadron, RE	65-69
3rd Field Squadron, RE	39-41, 65-70
4th Field Squadron, RE	51-55
5th Field Squadron, RE	43-47
6th Field Squadron, RE	57-59
7th Field Squadron, RE	32-37, 105
8th Field Squadron, RE	43-47
9th Field Squadron, RE	58, 59
10th Field Squadron, RE	61-63
11th Field Squadron, RE	61, 62
12th Field Squadron, RE	73, 74
13th Field Squadron, RE	73-76
14th Field Squadron, RE	89-93
15th Field Squadron, RE	89-90
16th Field Squadron, RE	78, 79
17th Field Company, RE	78, 103
18th Field Squadron, RE	81, 82
19th Field Squadron, RE	81, 82
20th Field Squadron, RE	108
21st Field Squadron, RE	54
23rd Field Company, RE	99, 100
59th Field Company, RE	105
204th Field Company, RE	110, 111
225th Field Company, RE	105
238th Field Company, RE	99, 100
244th Field Company, RE	113
246th Field Company, RE	103
248th Field Company, RE	99, 100
253rd Field Company, RE	103
260th Field Company, RE	110, 111
278th Field Company, RE	107, 108
279th Field Company, RE	107, 108

BRITISH ARMY DIVISIONS IN WWII

Trevor Laing

Part II: Infantry and Motor Divisions

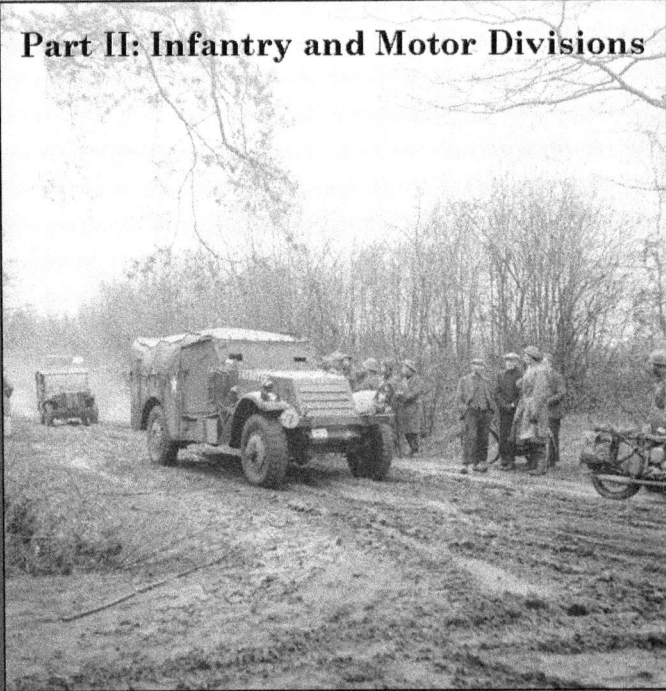

For publishing date see: www.tl219.com

BRITISH ARMY DIVISIONS IN WWII

Trevor Laing

Part III: Airborne, Anti-Aircraft, Calvary and County Divisions

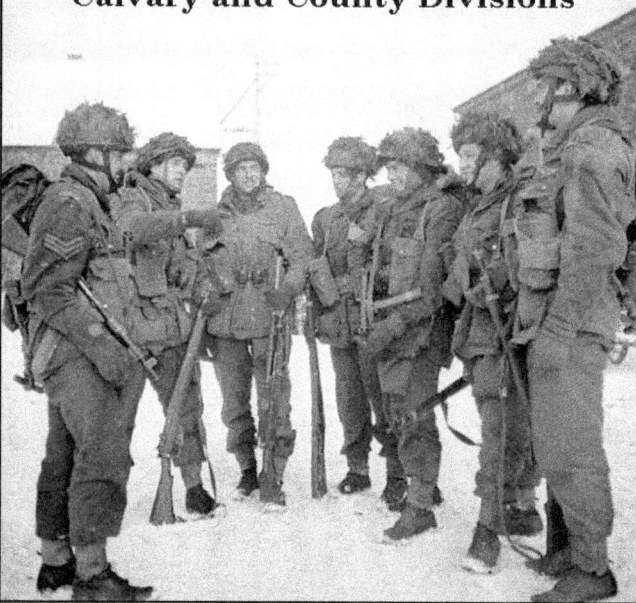

For publishing date see: www.tl219.com

Related Books by Travelogue 219:

www.tl219.com

A Token Force: The 261st Field Park Company Royal Engineers (Airborne) at Arnhem by John Sliz
ISBN: 978-0-9877404-6-5

Basic Function: The 4th Parachute Squadron, Royal Engineers at Arnhem by John Sliz
ISBN: 978-0-9783838-1-7

Bridging the Club Route: Guards Armoured Division's Engineers During Operation Market Garden by John Sliz
ISBN: 978-1-927679-14-2

Churchill's Warriors: Personal Stories of British Airborne Troops in the Second World War by Andy Johnston
ISBN: 978-1-927679-63-0

Commander Royal Engineers: The Headquarters of the Royal Engineers at Arnhem by John Sliz
ISBN: 978-1-92679-04-3

Engineers at the Bridge: The 1st Parachute Squadron Royal Engineers at Arnhem by John Sliz
ISBN: 978-0-9783838-4-8

Gales' Eyes Part I: Headquarters and the Brigades
by Carl Rymen
ISBN 978-1-927679-50-0

Gales' Eyes Part II: Support Units
by Carl Rymen
ISBN 978-1-927679-62-3

Officers at Arnhem An Examination of the Command Structure of the British 1st Airborne Division Which Fought at Arnhem in September 1944
by Trevor Laing
ISBN: 978-1-927679-27-2

The Wrong Side of the River: The Polish Engineer Company at Arnhem by John Sliz
ISBN: 978-09783838-0-0

www.ingramcontent.com/pod-product-compliance
Lightning Source LLC
Chambersburg PA
CBHW070810050426
42452CB00011B/1978